DATE DUE

3/21/97	

GAYLORD PRINTED IN U.S.A.

THE RISE OF URBAN AMERICA

THE NEIGHBORHOOD

A STUDY OF LOCAL LIFE

IN THE CITY OF COLUMBUS, OHIO

Roderick Duncan McKenzie

ARNO PRESS
&
The New York Times
NEW YORK • 1970

Reprint Edition 1970 by Arno Press Inc.

Reprinted from a copy in The Harvard College Library

LC# 71-112560
ISBN 0-405-02465-7

THE RISE OF URBAN AMERICA
ISBN for complete set 0-405-02430-4

Manufactured in the United States of America

The Neighborhood: A Study of Local Life in the City of Columbus, Ohio

By

RODERICK DUNCAN McKENZIE

THE UNIVERSITY OF CHICAGO PRESS
CHICAGO, ILLINOIS

Published February 1923

Composed and Printed By
The University of Chicago Press
Chicago, Illinois, U.S.A.

PREFACE

Several years have elapsed since this study was completed. The only reason for reprinting now in book form is to meet the Doctor's dissertation requirements of the University of Chicago. The modern city is in rapid process of change. The findings revealed in this study may now have but historic significance. The method employed, however, may possess elements of more permanent value.

It is almost beside the point to say that I am much indebted to the many students and friends in Columbus who so generously assisted in the field work connected with this study. I am, however, particularly obligated to my good friend and teacher, Dr. Robert E. Park, for his patient and able guidance throughout the entire work.

TABLE OF CONTENTS

LIST OF ILLUSTRATIONS

LIST OF TABLES

Reprinted from
The American Journal of Sociology, Vol. XXVII, September, 1921;
November, 1921; January, 1922; March, 1922; and May, 1922

THE AMERICAN
JOURNAL OF SOCIOLOGY

Volume XXVII SEPTEMBER 1921 Number 2

THE NEIGHBORHOOD: A STUDY OF LOCAL LIFE IN THE CITY OF COLUMBUS, OHIO

R. D. McKENZIE
University of Washington

ABSTRACT

City structure. Cities are usually classified according to size. They may be also classified according to the nature and organization of their leading industries. Land valuations in the forms of business, industrial, and residential utilities, largely determine the structure of the modern city. Every city has its central business district, located near the geographical center of the city. Sub-business districts tend to form at street-car crossings and around neighborhood institutions. The basic industries are usually located around the outskirts of the city's corporation, while manufacturing establishments employing women are usually located near the center of the city. Real estate values distribute a city's population into various residential sections of different economic and social status. Racial and nationality bonds tend to subgroup the population within the various economic areas. *Mobility of population.* The term implies the extent to which the individual varies his environment, either by change of residence or by use of secondary means of communication. The mobility of modern life facilitates disorganization of traditional group and institutional structures. It is a measure of progress, but at the same time aggravates many of our political and social problems. Change of residence is much more frequent among the lower economic classes in Columbus than among the well-to-do. But dependence upon local institutions is considerably greater in the poorer neighborhoods than in the better residential sections, on account of inability to use secondary means of communication.

PART I. LOCAL LIFE WITHIN THE CITY

I. CITY STRUCTURE

Columbus is a city of about 210,000 inhabitants, according to the latest census. There are forty-three other cities in the United States, which, from the point of view of population, fall in the same class.[1] Of these cities eleven are in the New England states, eight in the Middle Atlantic, seven in the East North Central, two in the West North Central, two in the Mountain, and five in the Pacific states.

Inasmuch as the modern city is largely an industrial institution it is important to know the nature of a city's leading industries. Eighteen of the cities in question have for their main industry the production of iron and steel products, eight have textiles and clothing, four lumber, three boots and shoes, three baking and confectionery, two publishing and printing, two preserving and canning, one rubber goods, one furniture, one jewelry, and one cotton-seed oil.[2]

These cities may again be classified according to the relative importance of their leading industries. Nine of the forty-four cities of this group are characterized by the national importance of their major industries.[3] For example, Patterson, New Jersey, Fall River, Lowell, and Lawrence, located in Massachusetts, belong to the textile and clothing group and have their industries organized on a nation-wide sale of products. Similarly, Akron with its rubber goods, Grand Rapids with its furniture, Youngstown with its iron and steel products, represent the type of city with a single dominant industry organized on a national scale. The majority of the cities in this group, however, are not characterized by a single outstanding industry but possess numerous small industries of approximately the same size, the larger part of their business being limited to local trading areas. Cities with this type of industrial life may be called diversified cities.[4] Columbus

[1] The estimated population of Columbus for 1916 was 209,722. It belongs to the third group of American cities, those having a population of 100,000 to 300,000. There was a total of forty-four cities in this group in 1916. *General Statistics of Cities* (1916).

[2] This classification was made from the *Census of Manufactures*, Vol. I (1914) and is based on census returns (1910). Undoubtedly in several instances the leading industry of 1910 is not the leading industry of today. The industry employing the greatest total number of employees was taken as the leading industry.

[3] Cities in which the major industry employed more than twice as many workers as the industry next in order, and more than the total listed for the classification, "all other industries" I have classified here, as "single-industry cities."

[4] See C. A. Beard, *American City Government* (1912), pp. 26–29, for a classification of types of American municipalities.

belongs in this latter class.[1] It has three relatively important types of industry: foundry and machine-shop products; the construction of cars, locomotives, and heavy machinery, and the manufacture of boots and shoes.

Most of our great cities are circular or star shaped unless directly modified by geographical peculiarities. This structure is due to the inherent nature of city development, when uncontrolled by conscious design. "Whatever the type of city, growth consists of movement away from the point of origin, and is of two kinds; central, or in all directions, and axial, or along the water courses, railroads and turnpikes which form the framework of cities."[2]

Columbus is shaped like a Greek cross. Its two leading thoroughfares, Broad and High streets, intersect at right angles near the junction of the Scioto and Olentangy rivers. High Street, the business backbone of the city, runs north and south for a distance of about nine miles within the corporation limits. Broad Street, on the other hand, runs east and west, or nearly so, and forms the arm of the cross. This street comprises part of the old Lincoln Highway. Topography has had something to do in determining the rough outlines of the city's structure. The junction of the two rivers just mentioned furnishes the basis for the crosslike appearance of the city. Expansion has followed the lines of least resistance along the south side of the Scioto River and the east bank of the Olentangy.

The distribution of business, industry, and population within the confines of any large city is determined by the operation of economic forces which tend to produce certain similarities of structure with respect to all big cities.

Generally speaking, the utility of land in the city falls into three classes: business utility, industrial utility, and residential utility. The areas devoted to these purposes are separated by more or less definite lines and are themselves

[1] Columbus, like almost every other city of its size, manufactures articles which are sold throughout the entire country, also in foreign lands, but Columbus is not dominated by any particular industry, nor does it have the habit of advertising in any of the national journals such as the *Post*, *Literary Digest*, etc.

[2] Richard M. Hurd, *Principles of City Land Values* (*Record and Guide*, *1903*). Adapted as a reading in Marshall, Wright, and Field, *Materials for the Study of Elementary Economics* (1913), p. 620.

subdivided according to the specific nature or class of use for each purpose. Business area for instance lies generally at the focus of local transportation routes or in other words at the point of intersection of the strongest lines of local

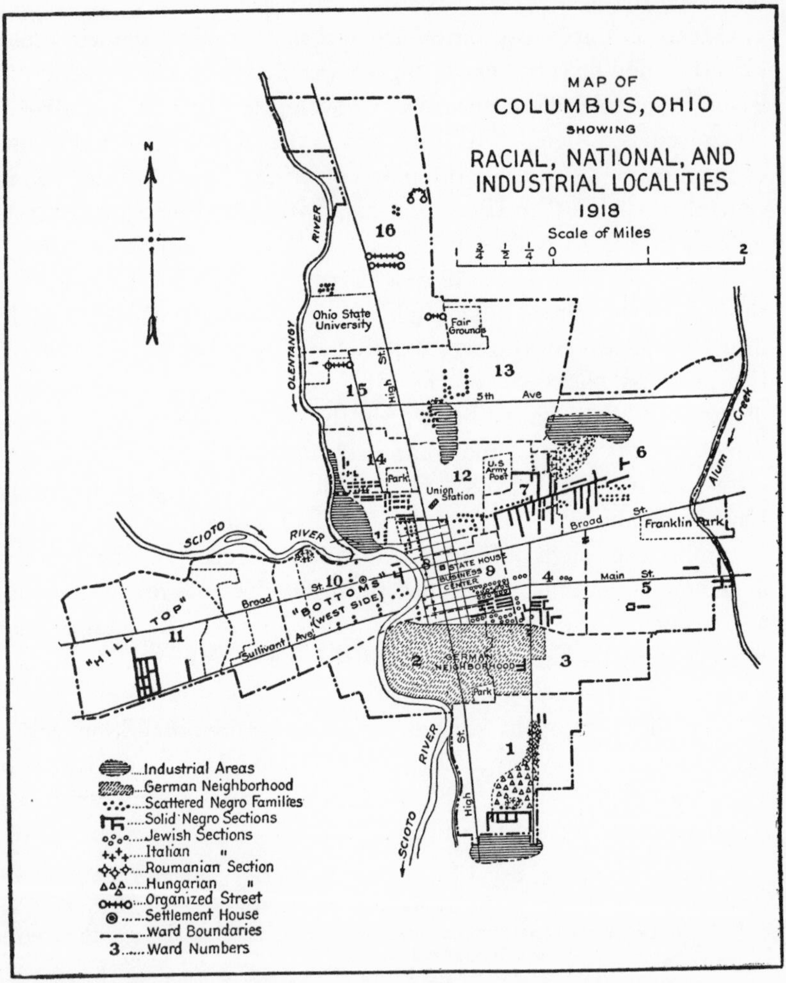

Map I

travel. This point is very often at the geographical center of the city which can be reached from all sections of the city with equal facility. The industrial area on the other hand has no one definite location, as has the business area. Depending largely on railroad facilities, it soon becomes scattered throughout all sections of the city, forcing its way from all directions in wedges almost to the business heart. There is generally no control and no concentration other than that offered by the railroad lines. To residential purposes is devoted the rest of the land in the city. This is generally of three classes: fine residential area; general residential area; and tenement area. The first of these preempts those sections of the city which have the greatest number of pleasing and natural advantages. The second, in general, lies along the thoroughfares and highways which have the best transportation facilities and also along such railroads as provide suburban transportation. The third class, the tenement areas, are generally found in the industrial regions and in the pockets or areas that lie between railroad lines and close to the center.[1]

The central business section of Columbus, as indicated on Map I, is located near the geographical center of the city. It comprises an area of about half a mile in length and three blocks in width, the central part of which is the junction of the two streets already mentioned. This is the corner of the State House grounds, also the site of the city's leading hotel. One does not *feel* that he is "down town" until he reaches this corner.[2]

Immediately surrounding the central business section of most cities is to be found a more or less disintegrated area, comprising wholesale establishments, low class hotels and apartment houses, second-hand stores, and cheap places of amusement. This region is usually inhabitated by a migratory class of people, such as day laborers, immigrants, and negroes. It also tends to become the rendezvous of the vicious and criminal classes.

The factors distributing values over the city's area by attracting or repulsing various utilities, are, in the case of residences, absence of nuisances, good approach, favorable transportation facilities, moderate elevation, and parks;

[1] E. H. Bennett, "Planning for Distribution of Industries," *Annals of the American Academy* (January, 1914), pp. 217–18.

[2] Referring to the defects of the round city John P. Fox, Secretary of the Transit Committee, City Club of New York, writes, "The round city, as found in America, tends to have a congested business center, with high buildings, high land values, high rents, congested streets and similar faults. It tends to require riding to and from work, especially if one wishes to live anywhere near the country. It requires too many radiating streets to reach surrounding territory, using more land than necessary. It makes it impossible to build one adequate rapid transit line to serve all the central district and the residence sections. It buries most people in its midst too far from the country, the latter being reached only by riding, which many poor people cannot afford to do."—"Relation between Transit and Housing," *Annals of the American Academy* (January, 1914), p. 160.

in the case of retail shops, passing street traffic, with a tendency toward proximity to their customer's residences; in the case of retail wholesalers and light manufacturing, proximity to the retail stores which are their customers; in the case of heavy wholesaling or manufacturing, proximity to transportation; and in the case of public or semi-public buildings, for historical reasons, proximity to the old business center; the land that is finally left being filled in with mingled cheap utilities, parasites of the stronger utilities, which give a low earning power to land otherwise valueless.[1]

Such a disintegrated area is quite conspicuous in the city of Columbus. Surrounding the main business section on all sides for a distance of from one to a dozen blocks there is a black and grimy area unfit for human habitation. Here cheap boarding houses and questionable hotels are wedged in between large warehouses and wholesale establishments. This region is very largely given over to colored people and poor whites.[2] Prior to the suppression of segregated vice in the city a considerable part of this section was occupied by keepers of immoral resorts. The eastern part of this district contained, in the early days, the homes of many of the wealthiest residents of the city. However, with the expansion of business and the development of modern means of transit, the well-to-do moved farther east along Broad Street, leaving their now obsolete homes to be used as places of business or to be subdivided into cheap apartments for the poor.

Most of our cities, due to their rapid growth, have districts that are going through a transition from resident districts to factory and business districts. Rents from dwellings are decreasing, while land value is greatly increasing. The owners of many of these homes, foreseeing the opportunity to sell the land for business purposes in one year or ten years, will not repair or improve their houses, because they argue it would be a waste to put more money in the houses that will in themselves bring no return when selling the land.[3]

The primary industries of most cities tend to be located near the outskirts of the city's corporation, along water fronts and

[1] Richard M. Hurd, *op. cit.*, p. 620.

[2] In his study of 4,500 employees in factories located in Norwood and Oakley, suburbs of Cincinnati, Graham Romeyn Taylor found that "nearly half, or 44.68 per cent, live in thickly populated parts of down-town Cincinnati, five miles from their work."—*Satellite Cities*, p. 97.

[3] Mildred Chadsey, "The Old House as a Social Problem," *Annals of the American Academy* (January, 1914), p. 87.

railroad tracks. Smaller industries, especially those employing women and unskilled labor, seek low-priced areas near street-car lines and so may be located in almost any part of the city. Around the primary industries independent communities develop which have a life of their own distinct from the rest of the city, such, for example, as the stockyard district of Chicago. Subcommunities of another type, due to the difference of population selection, form around any important center, such as a university, park, school, or other public institution.

Transfer points, owing to concentration of daily streams of people and consequent opportunity for shops, are strategic points in a city's area, creating business subcenters, whose prospects of increasing values are limited only by the number and quality of the people likely to utilize them. As examples, note the marked effect of transfers in New York at Broadway and 34th Street, Madison Avenue and 59th Street, Lexington Avenue and 59th Street; also in New Haven at Chapel and Church streets; in Denver at 15th and Lawrence streets; and many transfer points in the outlying districts of Chicago.[1]

Columbus has three significant industrial communities. One is located in the twelfth ward and contains the plants of the Jeffrey Manufacturing Company, which employs about 4,000 men, and the High Malleable Company, which employs about 700 men. The second industrial area lies along the Scioto River, extending from First Avenue down to the center of the city. In this district are the plants of the Lamneck Furnace Company, the Nye and Sons Stove Company, and the Hulse Furniture Company. The third industrial section is found in the south end of Columbus. Here are the large steel industries of the city, including the Buckeye Steel Casting Company, the Columbus Branch of the American Rolling Mill Company, the Seagraves Manufacturing Company, and others. In addition to these manufacturing areas the shops of the different railroads form other industrial communities. The Hocking Valley Shops are located in a bend of the Scioto River in the western part of Ward 2, making this section of the ward much less stable than the remaining German part of it which lies east of High Street. Similarly the large Pennslyvania Shops, located a short distance northeast of the United States barracks, account for the mixed foreign and negro section found there.

[1] Richard M. Hurd, *op. cit.*, p. 622.

Each of these industrial areas has a more or less distinctive community life of its own. The residents of these communities are very largely people who work in the nearby industries. While their economic status is that of the day-laboring class still their population elements comprise a mixture of practically all racial and national stocks. There is a distinct tendency, as may be seen by Map I, for the different racial and linguistic groups to form little colonies within these industrial communities. This is especially noticeable with respect to the industrial area surrounding the South Columbus Steel Works. This is a motley district, practically every street represents a different racial or national aggregation.

The population of any city is distributed according to economic status into residential areas of various rental or real estate values. Family income tends to segregate the population of a city into different economic districts much the same as the price of tickets at a theater divides the audience into several different strata of economic and social distinction.

> The main consideration in the individual selection of a residence location is the desire to live among one's friends or among those whom one desires to have for friends; for which reason there will be as many residence neighborhoods in the city as there are social strata.[1]

In order to bring into relief the various levels of economic distribution of the population of Columbus a measure of comparative economic status was sought. It was finally decided to take the average per elector tax returns on household furniture as a standard of rating. Household furniture returns are listed from the home address rather than from the down-town office, and, therefore, furnish a territorial distribution of this sort of property. The returns were calculated by wards and the totals divided by the number of registered electors for the same year in each ward.[2]

The measure of economic status here adopted is not without its shortcomings. In the first place the ward is not a homogeneous economic area. It frequently includes the extremes of wealth and

[1] Richard M. Hurd, *op. cit.*, p. 621.

[2] The ward totals were divided by the number of registered electors rather than by the number of householders, inasmuch as each householder is allowed one hundred dollars tax exemption on furniture, and, therefore, in the lower economic regions only a small percentage of the families made returns at all.

poverty. This is true, for example, with respect to the sixth ward, the eastern end of which contains some of the most luxuriant homes in the city, while the western corner represents a broken-down colored section. But, on the whole, the classification of

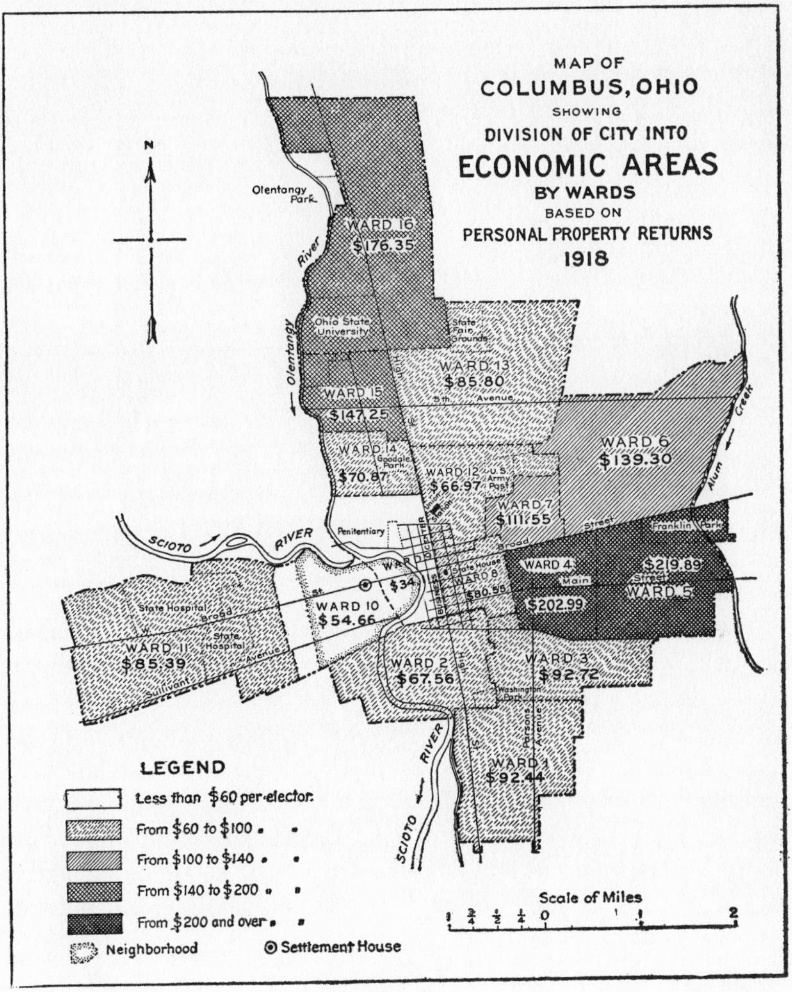

Map II

wards, as determined by this form of measurement, corresponds almost precisely with the common-sense rating as based on general observation. The foregoing map (Map II) indicates the results of this study.

The first impression gained from an examination of this map will be the striking difference in economic status of the various wards in the city. Wards 4 and 5 with their economic status of $202 and $219 respectively, stand in bold contrast to Wards 9 and 10 whose per elector status is less than one quarter as great. The latter wards, as may be seen by Map III (p. 163) are also the most mobile sections of the city. Wards 15 and 16 comprise the university district and represent the middle class type of home. The relatively low rating of Ward 11 is due to the presence of a large negro colony located near its southern border, also to a disintegrated neighborhood lying north of the State Hospital for the Insane. On the other hand, Ward 1 is probably rated a bit too high. This is a foreign locality surrounding the South Columbus Steel Works and our measure of economic status applies merely to citizens.

Racial and national sentiments tend to subgroup the population of the different economic areas of a city into more intimate social divisions. "Every great city has its racial colonies, like the Chinatowns of San Francisco and New York, the Little Sicily of Chicago, and various other less pronounced types."[1] Columbus has several such racial and national colonies, each with a more or less distinct social life of its own.

The colored population,[2] as may be noted on Map I (p. 148), is, in general, distributed around the periphery of the main business section, along the river flood plains, near the railroad tracks, and around the industrial plants. Most of Ward 9 is inhabitated by colored people. During the past few years the colored families, especially the new arrivals from the South, have been pushing their way out into Ward 14, driving the Italians, who previously occupied this territory, still farther north. The northern boundary line of Ward 9, Goodale Street, is now almost entirely inhabitated

[1] Robert E. Park, "The City: Suggestions for the Investigation of Human Behavior in the City Environment," *American Journal of Sociology*, XX, 582.

[2] In 1910 Columbus had a colored population of 12,739, which, when compared with the total population of the city, constituted at that time a higher percentage of negroes than was to be found in any other city in the state. Moreover this number has been greatly augmented by the influx of negroes from the South during the past few years.

by negroes. The river end of this street, together with the immediately surrounding territory, was originally known as "Fly Town," receiving this name on account of the migratory tendencies of workers employed in the nearby factories, also on account of the lawlessness of the place. In this section the Godman Guild Social Settlement House is located.

The largest colored community in the city lies just east of the central business district. This community includes practically all of Ward 7 with the exception of a few streets on which are located some of the best residences in the city. It also extends into the southwestern corner of Ward 6, the eastern half of Ward 8, and the western part of Ward 4. The central part of this colored community lies north of Long Street between Seventeenth Street and Taylor Avenue. This region is undisputably surrendered to negroes. It is a city of blacks within the larger community. Here are found colored policemen, colored hotels, stores, churches, poolrooms, picture theaters, as well as separate colored schools. The colored people have their own local organizations such as lodges, war-relief clubs, and a political organization called "The Negro Republican League."

Of the minor negro colonies indicated on Map I attention should be called to the one in the extreme south end of the city, adjoining the steel plants; to the colored neighborhood in the eleventh ward, reference to which will be made later; to the colored district surrounding the Jeffrey Manufacturing Plant in Ward 12, and to the smaller colored localities adjoining the university campus.

Columbus has one large Jewish colony, lying a few blocks east of the southern end of the main business section of the city. This district is bounded on the north by Rich Street, on the east by Parsons Avenue, on the south by Livingston Avenue, and on the west by Grant Street. In this quadrangle, comprising about twelve city blocks, there is located the Jewish Schonthal Community House, Temple Israel, the Agudas, Achim Synagogue, Tiffereth Israel Synagogue, the Beth Jacob Synagogue, the Ahavath Sholen Synagogue, and the Jewish Progress Club. The area described, however, is not inhabitated entirely by Hebrews. The population is a mixture of colored and Jewish people. This is the home of the Orthodox Jews of Columbus.[1] The so-called "Reformed" Jews, which include, as a rule, the Jews of German nationality, are dispersed along the eastern section of the city in the better residential district between Broad Street and Bryden Road.

The renowned German section[2] of the city extends along South High Street from Livingston Avenue as far south as Washington Park, bounded on the east by Parsons Avenue, and on the west by the Hocking Valley tracks. It comprises an area of about a square mile and falls, for the most part, within the second ward. Many of the most prominent of the old German families reside along High Street south of Livingston Avenue. Practically all of these families own their homes and many of them have resided here for over thirty years. The whole community, just outlined, is fundamentally German. The dwellings represent the typical German village structure, built close up to the sidewalk, with garden space and chicken house in the rear. Many of the alleys are lined with small residences. Frequently the owner of a fine home will have a small building on the rear of his lot occupied by a tenant family. The shops, churches, and other public places of this district are owned and operated by Germans, and the German language is used almost exclusively.

Lying immediately south of this German neighborhood and extending to the southern limits of the city is a mixed foreign district, inhabitated by Austrians, Lithuanians, Hungarians, and Italians.

II. MOBILITY

"The city is the spectroscope of society; it analyzes and sifts the population, separating and classifying the diverse elements."[3]

Mobility of population may be considered under three heads: change of residence from one community to another, change of

[1] This is the historic Jewish neighborhood of Columbus and is noted for the solidarity of its local life. Graham Taylor says, ". . . . The family-like fellowships persistently growing out of and around the Jewish synagogue, which is the most ancient type of the neighborhood still surviving, perpetuate the spirit of neighborliness and give it more or less flexible, but long accepted, forms of development."—*Religion in Social Action* (1913), p. 149.

[2] According to the 1910 Census, Columbus had 5,722 foreign-born Germans, which was the largest single foreign-born nationality in the city (*Thirteenth Census of United States*, III, 428).

[3] A. F. Weber, *The Growth of Cities in the Nineteenth Century* (1899), p. 442.

residence from one neighborhood to another within the community, and mobility without change of residence.[1] The official sources of information on these subjects are very inadequate. The census reports furnish data concerning nationality and interstate migrations,[2] but aside from that we know nothing about the movements of people from one community to another,[3] much less the movements that take place within the community itself.

That the mobility of modern life is intimately connected with many of our social problems there is general consensus of opinion. Assuming that a reasonable amount of mobility is both inevitable and desirable, nevertheless it is unquestionably true that the excessive population movements of modern times are fraught with many serious consequences.

Perhaps the most obvious effect of the mobility of the population within a city is the striking instability of local life. Neighborhoods are in a constant process of change; some improving, others deteriorating. Changes in incomes and rents are almost immediately registered in change of family domicile. Strengthened economic status usually implies the movement of a family from a poorer to a better neighborhood, while weakened economic status means that the family must retire to a cheaper and less desirable district.[4] So in every city we have two general types of neighbor-

[1] Robert E. Park says, ... "Mobility in an individual or in a population is measured, not merely by change of location, but rather by the number and variety of the stimulations to which the individual or the population responds. Mobility depends, not merely upon transportation, but upon communication."—*American Journal of Sociology*, XX, 589.

[2] The 1910 Census records the percentage of the population of each state born within the state. This gives a general impression of the relative mobility of the different states. The percentage of people born within the state in which they were counted varies from 94.7 for North Carolina to 21.8 for Wyoming. Ohio is above the average in stability with a percentage of native born of 74.4 (*Thirteenth Census of United States*, I, 712).

[3] See Bucher's *Industrial Evolution* (Wickett translation), chap. x, for an interesting study of internal migrations of population in Germany. He shows that of the population of Prussia, in 1880, 57.6 per cent were born in the municipality where enumerated (p. 354), and for Bavaria (1871) 61.2 per cent (p. 355).

[4] "A study of five hundred families who, in 1913, moved from one home to another has clearly shown that in 63 per cent of the cases poorer accommodations were secured because of a recent change in the family income which caused a necessary change in the amount of rent that could be spared."—Carol Aronovici, *Housing and the Housing Problem* (1920), p. 20.

hood; the one whose inhabitants have located there on the basis of personal choice, and the other whose inhabitants have located there as the result of economic compulsion. The former, as we shall see later, contains the possibilities for the development of neighborhood sentiment and organization, while the latter lacks the necessary elements for reconstruction.

Rapid community turnover also plays havoc with local standards and neighborhood mores. It is impossible to have an efficient local opinion in a neighborhood where the people are in constant move. It has repeatedly been affirmed by students of society that the decay of local standards is a pertinent cause of moral laxness and disorderliness.

> We are dependent for moral health upon intimate association with a group of some sort, usually consisting of our family, neighbors, and other friends. It is the interchange of ideas and feelings with this group, and a constant sense of its opinions that makes standards of right and wrong seem real to us. . . . . When we move to town, or go to another country, or get into a different social class, or adopt ideas that alienate us from our former associates, it is not at all certain that we shall form new relations equally intimate and cogent with the old. A common result, therefore, is a partial moral isolation and atrophy of moral sense. If the causes of change are at all general we may have great populations made up largely of such displaced units, a kind of "anarchy of spirits" among whom there is no ethos or settled system of moral life at all, only a confused outbreak of impulses, better or worse.[1]

The flux of modern life also intensifies all problems connected with government, national, state, or local. The fact that we have a residence qualification for voting leaves an increasingly large number every year of disfranchised citizens. This too applies especially to a class, the migrant laborer, which has no other means of participation in social control.

Our distinguished critic, James Bryce, drew attention years ago to the relation between mobility and government.

> In no state of the union is the bulk of the population so fixed in its residence as everywhere in Europe; in many it is almost nomadic. Except in some of the stagnant districts of the South, nobody feels rooted to the soil. Here today and gone tomorrow, he cannot readily contract habits of trustful dependence on his neighbors. Community of interest, or of belief in such a cause

[1] C. H. Cooley, *Social Process*, pp. 180–81.

as temperance, or protection for native industry, unites him for a time with others similarly minded, but congenial spirits seldom live long enough together to form a school or type of local opinion which develops strength and becomes a proselytizing force. Perhaps this tends to prevent the growth of variety of opinion. When a man arises with some power of original thought in politics, he is feeble if isolated, and is depressed by his insignificance, whereas if he grows up in a favorable soil with sympathetic minds around him, whom he can in prolonged intercourse permeate with his ideas, he learns to speak with confidence and soars on the wings of his disciples. One who considers the variety of conditions under which men live in America may certainly find ground for surprise that there should be so few independent schools of opinion.

Students of municipal government are constantly calling attention to the difficulty of creating interest in municipal affairs among a people who are in constant move.[2] Stability of residence, as a rule, implies home ownership, which in turn gives rise to local sentiment and interest in neighborhood surroundings. In a region where the population is continually shifting there is little opportunity for the development of neighborhood sentiment, and as a result, local concerns are usually left to take care of themselves. It is hard to develop interest in neighborhood affairs among families who are the while conscious of the temporary nature of their domicile within the district.

The problems which the mobility of population presents to political reformers are likewise common to social workers in other fields. Organizations dealing with delinquency and dependency are hampered in their efforts by the frequent movements of their "cases."[3] Similarly the church, trade union, and other voluntary forms of association lose in their efficiency through the rapid turnover of their local membership lists.[4]

[1] *American Commonwealth*, II (1907), 289–90.

[2] Hart (*Actual Government*, pp. 210-11) points out that the American habit of moving is an important cause of bad city government. Goodwin in his *Municipal Government*, p. 26, also emphasizes the relation of population movement to the problem of local government.

[3] In a study of 324 newly "closed" cases, in the records of the Social Welfare League of Seattle, it was found that the average length of time the families were under the jurisdiction of the organization was five months; and the average number of changes of residence during that period was 2.2. Moreover, 45.8 per cent of the cases were closed because the family had moved away from the city.

[4] In a study made of 2,049 resignations from the Seattle Chamber of Commerce (June, 1917, to December, 1920), Mr. Suen Chen, a student in sociology, discovered

In considering the general causes of the present mobility of population it is important to view the subject from both its psychological and its social aspects. Thomas and Znaniecki have grouped the dominant individual wishes or desires into four general classes: "the desire for recognition or status; the desire for safety or security; the desire for power; the desire for new experiences."[1] It is of course obvious that the relative strength of these different desires varies in different individuals and at different ages in the same individual. E. L. Thorndike says, "old age, femaleness, and physical weakness" . . . . seem to favor "the long familiar physical and social environment," while "adolescence, maleness, and energy"[2] seem to be combined with the roaming disposition.

Of the four types of desires just mentioned the desires for security and recognition find their chief satisfactions in the solidarity and intimacy of the small local group; while the desires for power and new experience attain their fullest fruition in a wider social milieu. The rigoristic codes of the small stable community have never afforded adequate satisfaction to the human impulses of the more energetic members of the group. The solidarity of the primitive neighborhood group was undoubtedly, to a greater extent, the product of a hostile external environment rather than the result of spontaneous human impulses. As Stuckenberg says, "Frequently the inherent qualities of men have less power to unite than the desire to antagonize what is averse to them. . . . . Prejudice, hatred, and opposition are powerful factors in association."[3]

---

that 764 or 37.3 per cent of those resigning had been members of the organization less than one year; 787 or 38.3 per cent had been members more than one year but less than two years; 328 or 16.1 per cent had been members more than two years but less than three years; while the remaining 170 or 8.1 per cent had been members three years or more. Moreover, 604 or 29.4 per cent of the total number resigning gave as their reason for leaving the organization change of residence to another community.

The present membership of the Seattle Chamber of Commerce (December, 1920) is 3,034; of this number 634 or 20.9 per cent have been members for one year or less; 1,197 or 39.4 per cent have been members for two years or less; and 1,517 or half the total number have been members for three years or less.

[1] *The Polish Peasant in Europe and America* (1918), I, 73.

[2] *Original Nature of Man*, I (1913), 56.

[3] *Sociology, the Science of Human Society*, I, 86.

Adam Smith contrasts the strong clan-feeling which still in the eighteenth century prevailed among the Scotch Highlanders with the little regard felt for remote relatives by the English, and observes that in countries where the authority of the law is not sufficiently strong to give security to every member of the State the different branches of the same family choose to live in the neighborhood of one another, their association being frequently necessary for their common defence: whereas in a country like England, where the authority of the law was well established, "the descendants of the same family, having no such motive for keeping together, naturally separate and disperse, as interest or inclination may direct."[1]

On the social side it is scarcely necessary to draw attention to the leading causes of intercommunity migration. The sudden change from a predominantly agricultural to a predominantly industrial society has occasioned a mobility of life unknown before. As long as the soil furnished the chief basis of economic income man was obliged to live a comparatively stable life in a fixed and definite locality. With the development of the modern capitalistic régime, the presence of the individual is no longer necessary to insure the productivity and security of his property. He may now, if he choses, invest his savings in interest-bearing securities which require neither his personal presence nor his attention to insure an income. He is thus left free to live, if he so desires, a nomad life.[2] Of course all classes in society are not equally free to move about. The middle-class tradesman and many of the professional groups are more or less tied to definite localities by the very nature of their work. On the other hand, the well-to-do and the day-laborer are free to move almost at will.

Our modern factory system is the chief cause of the present migratory tendencies of the wage-earning class. In an open labor market with employers competing with one another in their demands for labor, the wage earner is fast becoming a sort of tourist who spends but a short period in each community during his trip around the country.

Seasonal or intermittent occupations, temporary jobs, commercial depressions, occasional unemployment, and a general sense of the lack of permanency

[1] E. Westermarck, *Moral Ideas*, II (1908), 223.

[2] See Godkin, *Problems of Modern Democracy*, pp. 180 ff., for a brief discussion of this subject.

in the tenure of their industrial positions, pull settled families up by the roots and seldom leave them long enough in one place to take root again. Our manual workers are more and more transient. Many among them are forced to become tramping families.[1]

Moreover, change of residence from one section to another within the community is quite as disturbing to neighborhood association as is movement from one community to another. In order to get an idea of the comparative mobility of the population of the various local areas in Columbus, a study was made of the changes in the lists of the registered electors during the period of one year. The records of each year's registration are listed by precincts by the city's Board of Elections. The 1917 list of names was compared with the 1918 list, and the percentage of names per precinct of the 1917 list that reappeared in the 1918 list was taken as a measure of the relative stability of the precinct. For example, if a certain precinct had 100 registered electors for 1917 and only 75 of these names reappeared in the 1918 list the percentage stability of that precinct would be rated as 75. The city is divided into 262 precincts, each of which comprises about two or three blocks. The average registered electorate per precinct was, in 1918, 175. From this small geographical unit it is possible to get a rather intimate knowledge of the extent of local mobility of population.

Taking the city as a whole, only 58.6 per cent of the registered electors of 1917 re-registered in 1918. In other words, of the qualified voters of 1917, almost one-half failed to requalify to vote in their old precincts in 1918. The percentage of registration of electors varies greatly, of course, in the different sections of the city, precincts ranging from 31.0 per cent to 77.8 per cent. The most mobile precinct is located in Ward 9 near the Scioto River, while the most stable precinct lies in the center of the old German neighborhood in the northern corner of Ward 1. Map III gives the results of such tabulation by precincts for the entire city.

This map gives a picture of the relative stability of different sections of the city when judged by the single criterion of the

[1] Graham Taylor, *Religion in Social Action* (1913), pp. 143–44.

re-registration of electors. It does not show the actual extent of shifting of population within any particular spot. Failure to re-register is not definite proof that the elector has migrated from

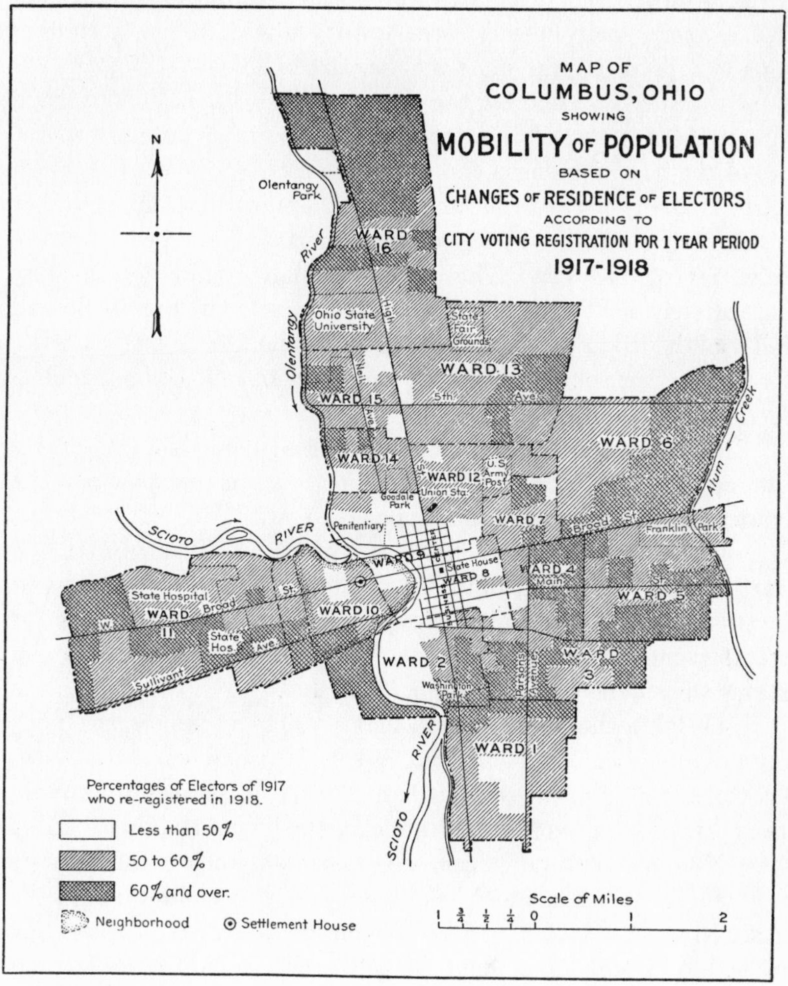

MAP III

the confines of his precinct. He may merely have omitted to perform this privilege of citizenship. On the other hand, movements of non-citizens are not recorded in this study. But, despite these limitations, I believe the method here employed furnishes an approximately true picture of the comparative population movements of different sections of the city.

It is quite evident from this map that the down-town section, including the main business area and its immediately surrounding territory, is by far the most mobile part of the city. But this is to be expected, considering the nature of this section. As we have already seen, most of the people living near the business center are of the boarding-house and cheap hotel class. The more stable parts of the city are to be found, for the most part, in the better residential districts, in the eastern, northern, and western extremities of the city. The large German neighborhood, lying immediately south of the main business section, practically all falls in the class of highest stability, while the industrial area, located farther south in Ward 1, comprises one of the most mobile sections of Columbus.

The correlation between stability and economic status is quite interesting. For ocular demonstration of this relationship the reader should compare Map III, page 163, with Map II, page 153. It must be borne in mind, however, that Map III is constructed on the basis of a small unit, the precinct, while Map II is based on the ward as the unit. Now taking the ward averages for stability and comparing them with the ward averages for economic status we get the result shown in Table I.

This table shows, in general, that stability varies directly with economic status. For example, Ward 9, which has the lowest economic status of all the wards in the city, has also the lowest re-registration of electors, which means the lowest stability. Likewise, Wards 8 and 12, which are considerably below the average in economic status, are also below the average in stability. On the other hand, Wards 4, 5, and 16 fall considerably above the average in stability, and rank high in economic status. Wards 2 and 3 appear to be exceptions; they have high stability and low economic status. But as we have already seen these wards contain the large stable German neighborhood, the residents of which, while home owners and relatively prosperous, maintain a lower standard of living than the average American of similar economic status.

Let us now examine the relation between mobility, dependency, and juvenile delinquency. The two spot maps (IV and V) facing page 166 show the geographical distribution of the official cases of dependency and juvenile delinquency for a one-year period, May, 1918, to May, 1919. As might be expected the majority of the dependency cases are segregated in the low economic areas surrounding the central business district. The colored cases form conspicuous groups near the railroad tracks and the river, also in the eastern part of the city near Franklin Park.

TABLE I

RELATION BETWEEN WARD STABILITY AND ECONOMIC STATUS

Ward	Average Re-registration per Ward (per cent)	Average Economic Status per Ward
9	43.7	$ 34.11
8	44.4	80.55
12	50.6	66.97
15	53.7	147.25
13	57.7	85.80
14	57.7	70.87
1	60.4	92.44
10	60.6	54.66
7	60.6	111.55
6	61.9	139.30
2	62.9	67.56
16	63.1	176.35
11	64.1	85.39
4	65.3	202.99
5	65.5	219.89
3	66.0	92.72

The most striking feature concerning the geographical distribution of juvenile delinquency is the rather even dispersion of cases throughout the entire city. Single streets or individual family groups rather than neighborhoods seem to form the nuclei for wayward children. There is, apparently, but slight correlation between the segregation of dependency and that of delinquency. Table II gives more exact presentation of the facts recorded in Maps IV and V.

It will be observed that Wards 8, 9, and 12, which comprise the central part of the city, and which rank highest in mobility, also rank high in extent of both dependency and delinquency; while

Wards 4, 5, 15, and 16 rank high in stability and have relatively little dependency or delinquency. However, the relation between mobility and dependency is much more conspicuous than the relation between mobility and delinquency. For example, Wards 13 and 14 have almost average stability but rank highest for the whole city in their percentages of juvenile delinquency. These two wards

TABLE II

WARD VARIATIONS IN STABILITY, DEPENDENCY, AND JUVENILE DELINQUENCY

Ward	Number of* Registered Voters for 1918	Stability†	Cases of Dependency‡		Cases of Delinquency	
			No.	Percentage	No.	Percentage
9	1757	43.7	82	4.67	27	1.54
8	2225	44.4	75	3.37	26	1.17
12	2062	50.6	94	4.56	25	1.21
15	2661	53.7	23	.86	12	.45
13	3062	57.7	51	1.67	49	1.60
14	2344	57.7	58	2.47	39	1.66
1	2950	60.4	58	1.79	45	1.53
10	2477	60.6	82	3.31	35	1.41
7	2721	60.6	44	1.62	23	.85
6	2995	61.9	65	2.17	32	1.07
2	2496	62.9	57	2.28	32	1.28
16	4540	63.1	24	.51	18	.39
11	3171	64.1	53	1.67	28	.88
4	2884	65.3	56	1.94	19	.66
5	3477	65.5	26	.74	12	.35
3	3635	66.0	45	1.24	34	.94
Total	45,457	....	893	....	456	....
Average for city	....	58.6	....	1.97	....	1.00

* The number of registered electors furnishes our only clue to the ward populations of the city, as the ward boundaries have been modified since the 1910 census was taken.

† The term "stability" implies here, as formerly, the percentage of the 1917 electors who re-registered in the same precincts in 1918.

‡ The cases of dependency and delinquency here recorded are known in the organizations concerned as "official cases," that is, they are the more permanent and serious cases with which the organizations have to deal.

happen to include industrial areas and have comparatively large colored and immigrant populations.

While our method of measuring mobility does not indicate whether the movements of families are from one community to another or from one neighborhood to another within the community, still a few sample cases seem to show the latter type of movement predominates. For instance, in Ward 9, out of the total 743 registered electors for 1917 whose names reappeared in the 1918 list, 141, or an average of 19.1 per cent, were listed with different street addresses within the confines of their respective precincts. When it is recalled that the precinct in Columbus comprises a very small area of but one or two city blocks, it is obvious that quite a considerable amount of mobility is from house to house within the same neighborhood. Another sounding was taken in Ward 16, an area of higher economic status. All the families in a single block were canvassed. Of the fifty-one families visited eleven had been on the street less than one year, thirty-two less than five years, and the remainder from five to ten years. Forty-one families had moved to the street from some other section of Columbus and of this number twenty-eight had moved to the street from the immediately surrounding neighborhood.

Again there is a type of mobility that is not indicated by change of residence, but which is almost as significant from the standpoint of neighborhood life. This is measured by the ability of the individual, due to modern methods of communication, to utilize the larger social environment afforded by the community as a whole. The automobile, street car, telephone, and press, together with increased leisure time, have all contributed greatly to the breakdown of neighborhood ties. Moreover, the disintegrating effects of these modern means of communication are not confined to the city alone. They have equal significance with reference to life in the country. To quote Cooley:

> In our own life the intimacy of the neighborhood has been broken up by the growth of an intricate mesh of wider contacts which leaves us strangers to people who live in the same house. And even in the country the same principle is at work, though less obviously, diminishing our economic and spiritual community with our neighbors.[1]

Warren Wilson says:

> In those states in which the trolley system has been extended into the country, for instance Ohio and Indiana, the process of weakening the country population has been hastened. Sunday becomes for country people a day for visiting the town and in great numbers they gather at the interurban stations. The city and town on Sunday is filled with careless, hurrying groups of visitors, sight-seers and callers, who have no such fixed interest as that

[1] *Social Organization* (1912), p. 26.

expressed in church-going or in substantial social processes. For the time being interurban trolley lines have dissipated the life of the country communities.

Referring to the use of the telephone and rural free delivery Wilson continues:

The old acquaintance and the intimate social relations of the country community have not been helped by the telephone: and along with the presence of aliens in the community, one quarter or one half or three quarters of the population, the telephone has had the effect of lowering the standards of intimacy and separating the households in the country from one another. The Rural Free Delivery has put the country people into the general world economy and for the time being has loosened the bonds of community life.[1]

It is an obvious fact that in isolated rural communities or backward city neighborhoods where the telephone has not become an instrument of common usage and where poverty restricts the use of secondary means of transportation, or where linguistic barriers prevent communication with the outside world; in such neighborhoods are to be found the best examples of the old neighborly forms of association. I shall, however, reserve for a later chapter the discussion of the influences of secondary means of communication upon social life in a city neighborhood.

[1] *The Evolution of the Country Community*, p. 128.

THE NEIGHBORHOOD: A STUDY OF LOCAL LIFE IN THE CITY OF COLUMBUS, OHIO

R. D. McKENZIE
University of Washington

ABSTRACT

Meaning of the concept neighborhood. It is difficult to define the neighborhood in the modern city. Interpretations of neighborhood made by various scholars seem to include three elements: spatial proximity to some focus of attention; physical or cultural differentiation from surrounding areas; intimacy of association among the inhabitants of the area. *History of the neighborhood.* Primitive peoples for the most part live in small territorial societies. The village community type of social organization represents the dominance of neighborhood over kinship as a bond of union. The ancient city was frequently but a federation of small locality groups. Even the modern city grows, as a rule, by the inclusion of small suburban communities, many of which retain their local self-consciousness for years after incorporation. *Elements of neighborhood association.* Cooley refers to the neighborhood as the universal nursery of the primary human ideals, such as kindness, loyalty, self-sacrifice, etc.; however hostility as well as mutual aid may flourish in neighborhood association. *Common sense conception of city neighborhood.* Students in Columbus defined neighborhood as the small personal area immediately surrounding their homes. *Organized neighborhoods in Columbus.* Several different streets of the city have developed local organizations for the promotion of local interests, such as street beautification, protection from industrial encroachments, and the encouragement of sociability. A study of these organizations shows that they are largely the products of the initiative and industry of a few individuals or families on each street.

III. THE NEIGHBORHOOD

The general effect of the continuous sifting and sorting of a city's population, as we have seen in the foregoing chapters, is to produce a patchwork of local areas differentiated from one another by cultural, racial, or linguistic peculiarities. In common parlance such areas are usually designated as localities, districts, colonies, or neighborhoods. Since the neighborhood is one of our oldest social institutions and since it is again coming into the focus of attention of writers on urban questions,[1] let us briefly examine its applicability to local life in the city environment.

Probably no other term is used so loosely or with such changing content as the term neighborhood, and very few concepts are more

[1] See, e.g., such recent books as M. P. Follett's *The New State* (1918), and John Daniel's *America via the Neighborhood* (1920).

difficult to define. The word neighborhood has two general connotations: physical proximity to a given object of attention, and intimacy of association among people living in close proximity to one another. On the flat plains of the agricultural states there are no objective marks by means of which the stranger can distinguish one rural neighborhood from another, yet almost any individual approached can give a very definite answer as to what constitutes his neighborhood; it simply embraces the area round about his home in which reside those families with whom he has intimate and direct personal relations.

In the city, on the other hand, there are very distinct objective differences between the various residential areas, but little or no personal acquaintance or group association among the families of any particular area. It is on account of these peculiarities of city life that we find so many different usages of the term neighborhood. Some writers are accustomed to use the word as implying mere physical proximity to a certain institution or topographical feature.[1] Others refer to the neighborhood as a cultural area,[2] sufficiently differentiated from the surrounding territory to be considered as a unit, while others again use the word in its traditional sense as implying intimacy of association[3] and personal acquaintance.

[1] Stuckenberg, *Sociology*, I (1903), 81.

[2] Park defines the neighborhood, "The City: Suggestions for the Investigation of Human Behavior in the City Environment" (*American Journal of Sociology*, XX, 579), as "a locality with sentiments, traditions, and a history of its own."

[3] Cooley lists the neighborhood as an example of a "primary group" (see *Social Organization*, chap. iii) and he defines a "primary group" elsewhere (*Amer. Jour. of Sociol.*, XXV, 327) as, "an *intimate* group, the intimacy covering a considerable period and resulting in a habitual sympathy, the mind of each being filled with a sense of the mind of the others, so that the group as a whole is the chief sphere of the social self for each individual in it of emulation, ambition, resentment, loyalty, etc." Kellogg in a rather vague way says, "the neighborhood is an intermediate group between the family and the city, among those communal organizations in which people *live* as distinct from purposeful organisations in which they *work* (*Charities and Correction* [1909], p. 176). Taylor (*Religion in Social Action*, p. 166) states that "the neighborhood is to be regarded as an extension of the home and the church, and is identified closely with both." Wood refers to the neighborhood (*Amer. Jour. of Sociol.*, XIX, 580), as "the most satisfactory and illuminating form of the social extension of personality, of the interlacing and comprehensive complex of the interplay of personalities; the social unit which can by its clear definition of outline, its inner organic completeness, its hair-trigger reactions, be fairly considered as functioning

one another" (R. M. Maciver, *Community*, p. 251). The same tendency is seen in Rome whose seven hills formed seven distinct neighborhoods. De Coulanges in *The Ancient City* shows that the Greek city was but a federation of local groups, each of which had its own religious and civil independence, and acted as a unit resenting interference on the part of the larger community. Of course similar tendencies toward local autonomy may be witnessed constantly in our own cities at the present time. Our cities grow by the inclusion of "satellite communities" and frequently such communities refuse to become absorbed in the larger corporations, and usually after surrendering their political autonomy retain for years a strong local consciousness and social independence.

In its traditional application the term neighborhood stood for rather definite group sentiments, which were the products of the intimate personal relations among the members of the small isolated communities of which society was formerly composed. The primary face-to-face associations of the traditional neighborhood group formed a universal nursery for what Cooley calls "the primary ideals," such as loyalty, truth, service, and kindness.[1]

Small homogeneous societies, such as the Russian *mir*, the Polish *zadruga*, or the isolated rural village, furnish our best examples of primary groups, that is of groups with a single set of definitions of life to which all the members adhere with an emotional unanimity. The ideas pertaining to group welfare have dominance over individual wishes, consequently there is a minimum amount of individuality when compared with life in a modern city. The solidarity of the traditional neighborhood is of the spontaneous unreflective type.[2] It is the result of common human nature responding to common stimuli. The relation between individuals of the group is that of equality. Referring to the early village life in this country, Sumner says (*op. cit.*, p. 296), "It is plain that *equality* is the prevailing characteristic of this society; its members are equal in fortune, in education, in descent (at least after a generation or two), in mode of life, in social standing, in range of ideas, in political importance, and in everything else which is social, and

[1] *Social Organization*, chap. iv.

[2] See James Mark Baldwin, *The Individual and Society*, chap. ii, 1911.

nobody made them so." Wood, in recounting the personal traits of our modern professional neighbor, the city boss, expresses a similar idea (*Amer. Jour. of Sociol.*, XIX, 580), "The local boss, however autocratic he may be in the larger sphere of the city with the power which he gets from the neighborhood, must always be in and of the local people: and he is always very careful not to try to deceive the local people so far as their distinctively local interests are concerned. It is hard to fool a neighborhood about its own neighborhood affairs." It is this insistence upon social equality among neighbors that deters the development of latent leadership in our rural communities.[1]

The solidarity of the traditional neighborhood included physical as well as social objects. The old swimming pool, the familiar hills and trees, the architecture and location of buildings, all function as sentimental attachments of the neighborhood. The individual becomes so closely identified with all these objects of early and intimate contact that they tend to form a part of the "extended self." Dr. W. I. Thomas,[2] in discussing the efforts of Germany to Prussianize Poland, says, "If the primary group is distinguished by face-to-face and sentimental relations I think it is correct to say that the land of the peasant was included in his group. And this land sentiment is the most important factor in the failure up to date of the plans of the colonization commission." Attachment for locality is even today a significant force in the segregation of a city's population.

Loyalty, self-sacrifice, and service are the natural products of the intimate personal neighborhood groups. As Tufts says, kindness suggests kinness, and applied originally to members of the "we-group" only.[3] Kropotkin, in his *Mutual Aid* furnishes us with a vast array of evidence concerning the reciprocal kindness of members of primitive communities. Sumner describes (quoted by Thomas, *Social Origins*, p. 79) the neighborly relations of the Yakuts of northern Siberia: "If one man's cow calves earlier than those of the others, custom requires that he shall share cream and

[1] See an article by G. Walter Fiske, *Publications of Amer. Sociol. Society*, XI, 59.

[2] *Amer. Jour. of Sociol.*, XIX, 632.

[3] Cf. Tufts, *Our Democracy, Its Origins and Its Tasks*, chap. iii.

milk with those neighbors who at that time have none." Cooley says (*Social Organization*, p. 38), "One is never more human, and, as a rule, never happier, than when he is sacrificing his narrow and merely private interest to the higher call of the congenial group." In his book *The American Town* (1906), p. 32, J. M. Williams describes the typical relationship between neighbors as follows: "A man must stand ready to help his neighbor as well as himself. Thus, when two woodsmen were working independently in adjoining wood-lots, each would impulsively run to the help of the other as he struggled to 'skid' a log upon a bob-sled. 'I'll help you and *you help me in return*' represents the complete relation. . . . . To be so 'close-fisted' as to fail of generosity in time of a neighbor's need was bad enough, but to fail to return, when needed, help generously extended, was meanness too abject for expression."

Of course social friction and petty jealousies are as much the products of neighborhood association as are self-sacrifice and mutual aid. As E. C. Hayes[1] says, "While instinctive cohesion is stronger in small groups, so also is personal friction greater, and the members of a small group much in spatial proximity must have more in common in order to render their union permanent and strong, than is required to bind together larger populations."

In order to get an expression of the common-sense conception of the neighborhood within the city, I had the students in my classes at Ohio State University, who were residents of Columbus, write answers to the following questions: "Draw a map of that part of your city which you consider to be your neighborhood. Indicate on the map the location of your home, and state the number of years you have lived there. Give your reasons for bounding your neighborhood as you do." The following statements are typical of the fifty-seven replies analyzed:

(1) These are the streets I traverse oftenest. (2) On these streets live the people with whom I am acquainted and associate. (3) When we get in this part of town we feel that we are getting near home. (4) I consider this my neighborhood because it includes the houses nearest my home and because I know most of the families in this vicinity very intimately. (5) These are the streets that I used to play in and I still know most of the families residing here.

[1] *Introduction to Sociology*, p. 76.

(6) To my mind the word neighborhood includes the people right around my house; it is the vicinity very near. (7) We speak of anything happening within a square of our home as being in our neighborhood but we do not know half of the people who live there. We have lived on this street six years. (8) I used to play with the children from most of these families [that is, families within an area of about a block and a half on the same street]; my small brother made me acquainted with others. I have lived here nine years. (9) Neighborhood to me means the people living in the same block we live in, those across the alley in the rear, and those living in the block across the street. (10) I consider the cross streets as the boundary of our neighborhood, the streets being so wide, especially where I live, that we do not recognize the people on the other side. I have lived here fourteen years. (11) I consider that this constitutes our neighborhood [an area of a couple of blocks] because these are the families that we come in contact with most frequently on the street car and at community gatherings. (12) I consider these particular streets my neighborhood because generally they are the only surrounding scene and the only people with whom we come in daily contact. (13) I have no particular reason for using this boundary as the boundary of our neighborhood except that it is the block in which we live, the families here are not of the sociable type; I have lived here four years. (14) I should say that my immediate neighborhood consists of the two southeast and southwest blocks; while the block at the northwest is also my neighborhood it is not my immediate neighborhood because we do not associate with these people and the spirit of the two factions is different. I have lived in this section for six years. (15) I consider my immediate neighborhood around the square S. to M. avenues since that is where I have lived the last five years. I think this is my neighborhood because we meet these people oftener and feel that we know them better.

From a consideration of these statements and from an examination of the maps which accompanied them, it is clear to me that the conception which the average city dweller holds of his own neighborhood is that of a very small area within the immediate vicinity of his home, the limits of which seem to be determined by the extent of his personal observations and daily contacts.

But in referring to neighborhoods in general in Columbus much larger areas seem to be implied, spatial proximity to some central focus of attention being the determining feature. For example it is local custom to speak of "Indianola," "Glen Echo," "The Hilltop," "West Side," etc., as various neighborhoods within the city, although each of these areas embraces many streets and contains thousands of people. What then is the city neighborhood? For certain administrative purposes it is important to consider these larger geographical expressions as units of neighborhood interest, while for other purposes, where intensity of social opinion counts, the smaller nuclei of common life may prove more effective units.

The segregation of the population within a city along racial, economic, social, and vocational lines, tends to give to different local areas at least an external coloring which enables one to draw more or less definite lines of demarkation between them. In the course of time these different areas acquire a sort of homogeneity and a historical continuity which develops a rudimentary sense of self-consciousness. This self-consciousness is usually enhanced if the area acquires a name designating its chief feature of attention, such as Niggertown, Flytown, Little Italy, etc. Such areas are, as a rule, in constant process of change, but since their selective influences attract about the same class of people from year to year their external aspects maintain a somewhat regular form. While districts of this sort vary greatly in size and in social solidarity, and while they may possess but few of the characteristics of the traditional neighborhood, nevertheless they possess sufficient significance from the standpoint of social selection, and have sufficient importance in community organization to warrant some such characterization as the term neighborhood.

If we consider the neighborhood then in this more general sense as representing a patch of common life within the larger community, which is sufficiently differentiated from the city as a whole to be thought of as a unit, we have several different types of neighborhoods represented in Columbus. Taking as our criterion for the classification of these neighborhoods, the chief element in population selection, we have three grades of economic neighborhoods,[1] that

[1] Consult Map II, p. 153, "Economic Areas in Columbus," for the locations of these different economic neighborhoods. It will be observed that, with but one exception, the south side, the economic status of the wards increases as one goes from the center out toward the periphery of the city. In fact the most exclusive neighborhoods all lie beyond the corporation limits. On the east side the suburban village of Bexley is the restricted area for the city's social élite. For many years Columbus has vainly sought to have this village enter the corporation, but up to date the villagers have preferred their local autonomy to the anonymity of city life. On the uplands, just beyond the western extremity of the city, are three other exclusive residential villages, Grand View Heights, Marble Cliff, and Upper Arlington. These villages are all of comparatively recent origin and the real estate restrictions limit the population to the wealthy home-owning class. Local consciousness is quite pronounced in all three and several experiments in community enterprises have been introduced, such as the local paper, the community church, the community kitchen, etc.

Another new residential section of the more exclusive type is fast developing just beyond the northern limits of the city. Many new additions have been opened up in this vicinity during the past few years and the Highlands east of the Olentangy River are rapidly becoming adorned with beautiful homes and picturesque gardens.

is, areas representing three fairly distinct economic divisions. These may be grouped as poor, middle class, and wealthy residential districts.

On the other hand, we have distinct racial and national groups where the chief elements in population selection are consciousness of kind, common language, and traditions. These are represented in Columbus by the large negro neighborhood on East Long Street, by the mixed Hebrew and colored neighborhood immediately east of the central part of the city, and by the homogeneous German neighborhood on South High Street.

In the third place we have the industrial neighborhood, in which reside the employees of a large industry, as, for example, the "South Side Neighborhood" surrounding the Columbus Steel Works, the chief factor in social selection being convenience to place of employment. Such neighborhoods usually represent a mixture of racial and national groups.

Again we may classify neighborhoods according to the status of their historical development into nascent, self-conscious, and disintegrating neighborhoods.[1] Like all other social groups, city neighborhoods are ever in a process of change. Fluctuations in rental and land values, due to the vacillation of city life, produce continuous movements of population from one section of the city to another, thus changing the economic and racial complexion of neighborhoods within a comparatively short space of time.[2]

The city neighborhood differs considerably from its traditional prototype in that it represents a much more selected social group. Economic, racial, and cultural forces, by distributing the population into different residential sections, give to the city neighborhood an external appearance of homogeneity that is not frequently found in small villages or rural neighborhoods—a homogeneity, however, as we shall see later, which is more apparent than real. Racial prejudice, national clannishness, and class conflict, all function as

[1] See Robert E. Park, *op. cit.*, p. 581.

[2] This is especially true with respect to immigrant neighborhoods. The economic progress of the immigrant is faster, as a rule, than that of the slum-dwelling American; consequently more immigrants than Americans graduate from the poorer neighborhoods. The district surrounding the Godman Guild Settlement House of Columbus has, according to the Settlement head, changed its immigrant population several times during the past decade.

social forces to give the city neighborhood what self-consciousness or solidarity it may possess.

IV. EXPERIMENTS IN NEIGHBORHOOD ORGANIZATION

The city of Columbus offers a number of rather unusual examples of the spontaneous development of local sentiment. In addition to the local improvement associations which have been organized in each of the larger local divisions of the city for the purpose of directing the general business interests, several streets have formed organizations to promote the interests of the residents on a single street or city block. Some of these organizations have interesting histories, and as experiments in the development of local sentiment are worthy of consideration. As far as can be ascertained these local organizations are all confined to the northern and western sections of the city, regions which are comparatively new, and for the most part occupied by home-owners.

Oakland Avenue Flower and Garden Club.[1]—Oakland Avenue is located near the center of the sixteenth ward, a few blocks north of the university campus. The part of the street that is organized extends from High Street on the west to Indianola Avenue on the east—a distance of about a quarter of a mile. The street is now thirteen years old, having been held in reserve by a real estate firm while the surrounding area was built up. A number of property restrictions have given a physical uniformity to the street and at the same time made for a selection of population. There is a building restriction ranging from $2,500 to $3,000 (pre-war prices) as a minimum cost per residence. The lots are wide and the homes are required to be built thirty feet back from the curb line, thus leaving a uniformly wide space for lawns and shrubs. Double dwellings and apartment houses are forbidden, also places of business.

The street became formally organized in the spring of 1912, the year of the Columbus Centennial. During that spring the Columbus Flower and Garden Club was formed in order to promote general interest in city beautification. A prize was offered for the

[1] See Map I, p. 148, for the locations of each of the neighborhoods described in this chapter.

best-kept street in the city. Under the capable direction of one of the leading residents of the street, the "Oakland Flower and Garden Club" was organized. Meetings of the residents were held in the Northwood School, located at the foot of the street, with the result that an enthusiastic program for street beautification was adopted. Large granite bowlders were erected at both ends of the street, giving it an individuality and prominence apart from the general neighborhood. Uniformity in design of lawn decoration was adopted with the result that, at the end of the year, the citizens of the street celebrated the jubilee of being the proud winners of the civic prize for the most beautiful street in the city. Meanwhile a local paper, the *Oakland Avenue News*, was periodically published and distributed to all the families on the street.

The enthusiasm engendered by this successful start has never quite died out although it has diminished in intensity and has required careful fanning on the part of a few indomitable spirits whose interest in the success of the undertaking has remained unabated. Although a comparatively stable street, the extent of change of residence has been one of the chief causes of the fluctuating interest in the organization. Of the eighty-five families whose names were listed in the street directory published in the *Oakland Avenue News* for September, 1913, thirty-eight had moved from the street before June, 1918—a period of five years.

The organization, designed primarily to promote street beautification, subsequently gave rise to many local activities of a social and neighborly nature, among which may be mentioned the admirable practice of sending floral tributes to neighbors in case of sickness or death; social picnics in which all families on the street participate, ladies' clubs, and a renowned bowling team, composed of male residents of the street.

Northwood Avenue Flower and Garden Club.—Northwood Avenue, which lies next to, and runs parallel with, the street just described, supports a similar organization. In fact I might have described the two streets together, were it not for the strong neighborly rivalry and unitary group character of each. Northwood has a physical basis for group life precisely similar to that of Oakland Avenue. It formed a part of the same real estate division and, therefore, was subjected to the same street restrictions. Its street organization was motivated by the same cause as that of Oakland Avenue but did not start off under quite such propitious circumstances. It took the Northwood residents a bit longer to get into teamlike action, but once started their organization has retained its health and vitality even better than that of its rival.

In the spring of 1917, with the assistance of some of my students, I made a brief study of the Northwood organization in order to get some clues respecting the nature of its group life. Every home on the street was visited with a brief questionnaire. I shall succinctly summarize here the results of our findings at that time. Questionnaires were filled out by fifty-one families. Of these eleven had been living on the street less than one year, thirty-two less than five years, and the remainder from five to ten years. All but three of the male heads of households were native-born Americans, and thirty-seven of the fifty-one male heads were born in the state of Ohio, six of whom were born in Columbus.

In reply to the question, "Why did you select this street as a place of residence?" fourteen said that it was on account of the attractive features of the street; another fourteen said it was because the house suited them; twenty could give no particular reason for their decision; while three maintained that their selection was due to the presence of friends and relatives on the street. Moreover, thirty-two families stated that they knew nothing of the street organization, prior to taking up residence there, while the remaining nineteen families were familiar with the social activities of the street and were more or less attracted to it on that account.

With respect to intimacy and personal acquaintance, nine families stated that they did not have even a speaking acquaintance with any other family on the street; thirty-five families reported that they had a speaking acquaintance with more than ten families on the street; while seven reported that they had a speaking acquaintance with more than thirty families. Six families stated that they were related, either by blood or marriage, to one or more other families on the street.

Of the male heads of households twelve reported no affiliation with community clubs or fraternal orders of any sort; twenty-three were members of but one fraternal organization; while sixteen belonged to two or more clubs. As regards religious affiliations, eleven different sects were represented, including membership or attendance at twenty-four different churches. Moreover, the leading bread winners were distributed among twenty-eight different forms of occupation, and of these only nine reported drawing any clientage from the immediate neighborhood.

An effort was made to sound the attitudes of the different householders toward their street organization and its leading functions. Of the fifty-one families, twenty stated that they had never attended any of the street's meetings; thirty-nine considered the organization definitely worth supporting; of these, twenty considered its main value to be the promotion of friendship and neighborly feeling, while the remaining nineteen valued it chiefly from the standpoint of its effect upon property values. Twelve families did not consider the organization worthy of support. Concerning the street practice of sending flowers to neighbors in the event of sickness or death, twenty-nine families reported having received such floral tributes, and all but four indicated positive appreciation of the custom and thought it should be continued.

Turning now to a consideration of the street paper, the *Northwood Avenue Bulletin*, this little paper has been published at irregular intervals ever since 1912. It is an unusually attractive little sheet containing many interesting views of the street and supplying information with respect to gardening and other matters of family interest. It also carries a page headed "Neighborhood Happenings," under which are listed news items pertaining to the people of the street. This paper represents the idea of one or two enthusiastic promoters and has been published at a loss to the few people most intimately concerned. An effort was made to ascertain the attitudes of the householders toward this paper, with the interesting result that forty-two of the fifty-one families were strong in their approval of it and considered that its publication should be continued.

Although a few of the families residing on this street at the time the above survey was made were opposed to any attempts to start "this small town stuff" in the city, still all but five maintained that it would cause them considerable regret to have to leave the street. Many families who stated that they had not the time to participate actively in the work of the street organization nevertheless indorsed the movement as being distinctly meritorious.

Ninth Avenue neighborhood.—Another interesting example of local manifestation of neighborhood sentiment and one which has been brought to the attention of the citizens of Columbus for the past decade or so is that of the residents of West Ninth Avenue. This little street, only two short blocks in length, is located close to the southwest corner of the university campus, in Ward 15. The Neil Avenue street-car line forms the eastern boundary of the neighborhood and the university farm borders it on the west.

Unlike the streets just described, the Ninth Avenue neighborhood supports no formal organization or street paper, but for years past the residents of the street have shown evidence of a distinct group feeling which reaches its highest culmination every year in a Fourth of July celebration. At this time the street is roped off from city traffic and all the residents of the block participate in a general street picnic, followed in the evening by a display of fireworks, which has become a tradition in the local life of the community. The street is much shorter than either of the others described, making it unnecessary to develop secondary means of communication, such as the local newspaper.

In physical appearance the street differs considerably from the surrounding area. In the first place it is built up with a distinctly superior type of residence from that found in the neighboring locality, the assessed value of the homes ranging from $4,000 to $15,000. The lawns are spacious and uniformly deep, lending a unitary character to the street.

In our brief study of this street we found that its group life depended very largely upon the energetic activities of a single family. The head of this household and his wife make a hobby of fostering neighborhood sentiment among the residents of the street. The meetings that are held to plan entertainments, etc., are usually conducted at this man's residence.

In addition to the club life that prevails among the residents of this street, such as picnics for the children, social activities of the women, and quoit games among the men, various other forms of collective action for local purposes have taken place. For instance, the street has persistently acted as a unit to keep its western vista over the university farm free from obstruction. It has also had several experiments in corporate action in fighting the intrusion of objectionable structures within its limits.

Glenmawr Avenue Improvement Association.—This little neighborhood is located in an attractive spot near the northern end of the sixteenth ward. The nature of this community and the purpose of its organization are well described in the following words of its secretary:

There is a park thirty-five feet wide and about one thousand feet long in the center of Glenmawr Avenue, and when the street was improved this space was left by the city with no improvements whatever, not even grass. It was necessary for the property owners to improve the condition of this park, and, therefore, the organization was formed with a view to beautifying the park and establishing a standard in the carrying forward of any improvements on the street, such as placing shade trees, constructing sidewalks, placing steps from the street to the yard, etc. Present membership, sixty-eight families. Any property owner on Glenmawr Avenue or any families renting property located on that street are eligible to become members.

The organization was able to have an ordinance passed through council permitting the placing of the sidewalks within two feet of the curb rather than five feet as is ordinarily required, which avoided the cutting off of the lawns, thus reducing the front yard space.

The park which was simply a bare space of ground, has been made level, fertilized, and a good standard of grass obtained. Seventy shade trees have been placed along the edge of the park and between these shrubbery has been placed. At the ends of the park flower beds with perennial flowers are maintained and gravel walks placed at intervals across the park to avoid persons having to cross from one side of the street to the other walking on the grass.

An ordinance was passed last fall by the Council of the City of Columbus, at the suggestion of the Association, requiring the installation of five cobblestone pillars, on which cluster lights will be installed through the center of the park. The grass in the park is taken care of by the residents without expense.

This Association also endeavors to have at their business meetings social entertainments for the residents of the street only, and by so doing have created a friendly feeling among the residents that could not otherwise have existed.

The money necessary to carry on the improvements that have been made in the park is obtained by assessment of the various residents of the street, the amount being collected without any hardship, and there is always money in the treasury to carry on improvements that might be authorized.[1]

The foregoing organization was formed in the spring of 1914, its meetings are held monthly at the home of one of the residents of the street. It serves an area of about two city blocks.

The Hilltop neighborhood.—The Hilltop is more than a neighborhood; it is a city within a city. It is a community of about 15,000 people, topographically separated from the city proper. It is an area complete in itself, having its own schools, churches, stores, shops, parks, fire-hall, social clubs, local newspaper, and improvement association, which is really equivalent to a chamber of commerce.

The Hilltop, as indicated on Map I, page 148, lies in the extreme western end of the city, about four miles west of the state's Capitol. As the name implies the Hilltop is a promontory rising considerably above the "flats" which separate it from the heart of the city. The division now comprises an area of several square miles and includes within its confines the State Hospital for the Insane.

Comparatively speaking the Hilltop is a new section of Columbus. Its chief development as a residential area has taken place during the past fifteen years, but once available for settlement its attractive topographical features made it an eldorado for the better class of home-seekers, with the result that it is now a city of new homes clustered around the few historic residences which graced the landscape in days gone by. Moreover, it is a region of considerable historic importance. Camp Chase of Civil War renown was located here, also the Confederate Cemetery, which lies in the southwestern part of the district.

Barring a small Italian neighborhood, located on McKinley Avenue at the rear of the Hospital for the Insane, and a larger colored colony located in the south along Sullivant Avenue, the Hilltop is primarily inhabitated by white American stock, the majority of whom are home-owners of the more prosperous class. An astonishingly large number of the leading public men of the city have their homes in this region, which fact doubtlessly accounts, in good measure at least, for the public spirit displayed among the residents of the Hilltop.

[1] Letter received from the secretary, January, 1920.

The negro neighborhood, just referred to, is the "fly in the ointment" with respect to the community pride of the people of the Hilltop. This colored section, covering an area of about six blocks, with a population of approximately 600 people, is not a recent development. A number of the colored families have resided in this spot for over thirty years, but a fresh influx of colored settlers arrived immediately after the Springfield riots a decade or so ago. A real estate dealer, devoid of "social vision," and "greedy for gain" sold his property to these people with the result that they are now fixtures in the community. Aside, however, from the acute social problems arising out of their presence in the schools, the colored people live to themselves and do not come in contact with the general social life of the community. The colored neighborhood has its own churches, stores, and motion-picture house, and the Camp Chase street-car line is used almost exclusively for transportation to and from the city. This colored neighborhood is one of the most orderly and progressive negro localities in the city. According to the estimate of one of the oldest colored residents, 75 per cent of the families own their homes; and it is a matter of local pride that "no one has been sent to the penitentiary from this district during the past twenty-five years."

The local consciousness of the residents of the Hilltop has manifested itself in many ways. In the first place a local paper called the *Hilltop News* is published weekly and read by more than "eight thousand Hilltoppers every week." This sheet is the "official organ of the Hilltop business men" and carries advertising and news items of local interest. It also serves as the official spokesman for the Hilltop Improvement Association, an organization of Hilltop residents designed to promote the welfare of the "Hilltop, its people, and their homes."

The Hilltop Improvement Association was organized in 1911 for the purpose just stated. It was promoted by a number of the most enterprising citizens of the community including one of the city's most prominent councilmen. No local organization of the city has been more active in the promotion of local interests, or has achieved more for the territory served than the Hilltop Improvement Association. Its field of activities has included negotiations with the city council for the procuring of local satisfactions, such as a recreation building, street-car accommodation, city deliveries, etc. It has also stimulated local pride in the care of property and in the repulsion of undesirable commercial encroachments, and at the same time has done much to engender a feeling of neighborliness and sociability among the people.

The community consciousness among the people of the Hilltop is due largely to the peculiar topographical features of the district which give it a unitary character quite distinct from the rest of the city. Moreover its conflict with the city proper in regard to flood protection measures relative to the flood area which separates it from the down-town district, has resulted in the development of the "we feeling" as contrasted with the rest of the city. In addition to this, the boosting attitude has been maintained by the comparatively large number of enterprising public citizens who have their homes in this district. These home-owners appreciate the significance of local community pride and consciously attempt to stimulate it in their locality.

Conclusions.—From a study of these and other experiments in neighborhood organization, I venture the following conclusions concerning neighborhood work in general. First, that neighborhood sentiment is most easily engendered where the physical basis of life affords a unitary character sufficient to differentiate the neighborhood from the larger community. Second, neighborhood sentiment thrives best where there is a homogeneity and stability of population accompanied by a high percentage of home ownership.[1] Third, other things being equal, the difficulty of maintaining local interest in local projects varies directly with the extent of territory covered and the number of families included. There is considerable evidence to show that a street more than two blocks in length tends to divide itself into subgroups, especially when two different street-car lines are used by the residents in communication

[1] According to our general test of stability for Columbus, i.e., the percentage of the 1917 electors who re-registered in their respective precincts in 1918, the organized neighborhoods just described rank comparatively high in stability. The average re-registration for the entire city was 58.6 per cent and for the most stable precinct 77.8 per cent. The precinct in which Oakland and Northwood avenues are located had a re-registration of 75.5 per cent, the Ninth Avenue precinct a re-registration of 69.1 per cent, and the Glenmawr precinct 64.9 per cent.

with the down-town district. Fourth, it may be stipulated that interest in the most obviously beneficial local enterprises, even under the most favorable conditions, is not as spontaneous and natural as many of our promoters of neighborhood enterprises seem to assume. In each experiment in neighborhood organization cited above, the interest in local affairs has been more or less artificially sustained by the "hard work" of a few energetic promoters.

Nevertheless, the value of such street organization cannot be doubted. No one who has visited any of the streets which have been described would question the superior merits of corporate action over the haphazard ways of traditional individualism. Aside from the social benefits accruing from local collective action, the effect on real estate values is in itself an important consideration, and one which real estate companies are beginning to appreciate.[1]

[1] I have been informed by several residents of the streets in question that they have been offered valuable concessions by real estate companies to promote similar organizations in new residential divisions which are now being put on the market.

THE NEIGHBORHOOD: A STUDY OF LOCAL LIFE IN THE CITY OF COLUMBUS, OHIO

R. D. McKENZIE
University of Washington

ABSTRACT

Description of neighborhood. The neighborhood is located in a flood plane near the center of the city. It comprises one of the oldest sections of the city and has been subject to periodic floods for years past. It is inhabited by working-class people, chiefly of American origin. *Mobility of neighborhood population.* The neighborhood serves as a reservoir for the city's human wastes. Families come and go in constant succession, and there are also frequent changes of residence from street to street within the neighborhood. There is a small nucleus, however, of stable superior families. The comparative absence of secondary means of communication, such as telephones and automobiles, makes the less mobile inhabitants—old men, women, and children—completely dependent upon the neighborhood institutions for their associational life. *Homes.* Most of the homes are obsolete both in structure and fixtures; scarcely 10 per cent have electric lights: about half of them are without baths or indoor toilets. Overcrowding is not prevalent except in alley houses. *Family life.* The neighborhood is a collectivity of very unlike family groups. Superior wholesome families are frequently found living next door to disorderly worthless people. Under such circumstances complete avoidance is practiced. The superior families usually represent early settlers who, on account of property ties, cannot leave their undesirable surroundings. *Economic condition.* This district represents the lowest economic level in the city. Home ownership is uncommon, and rents average less than fifteen dollars per month. However there are marked differences in the comparative economic status of adjoining families. Family groups in the depth of poverty are frequently found living side by side with families having comfortable incomes. *Leisure-time activities.* Most of the homes are ill-equipped with facilities for the fruitful utilization of leisure time. Reading materials are scant or wanting; musical instruments are found only in a small percentage of the homes. *Outdoor leisure-time activities.* The movies are the most popular form of commercialized recreation for mothers and children. The elder males find their chief enjoyment in the neighborhood saloons, while the youth, for the most part, patronize the uptown poolrooms and dance halls.

PART II. AN ANALYSIS OF A DISINTEGRATED CITY NEIGHBORHOOD

V. DESCRIPTION OF NEIGHBORHOOD

The following survey was undertaken upon the suggestion of the Brotherhood of the First Congregational Church of Columbus. For a number of years the church has been supporting a social settlement house, located on Broad Street, in the heart of the region west of the river. With a view to extending its activities on a more scientific and efficient scale, the Brotherhood voted in the spring of 1919 that a survey of the neighborhood surrounding the social settlement be made and a program of action outlined in conformity with the findings. The writer was selected to engineer the survey. The field work was done by advanced students in his classes in sociology at the state university.

The actual field work of the survey falls into three divisions: first, a house-to-house canvass of one thousand households located in the neighborhood just indicated. An attempt was made to

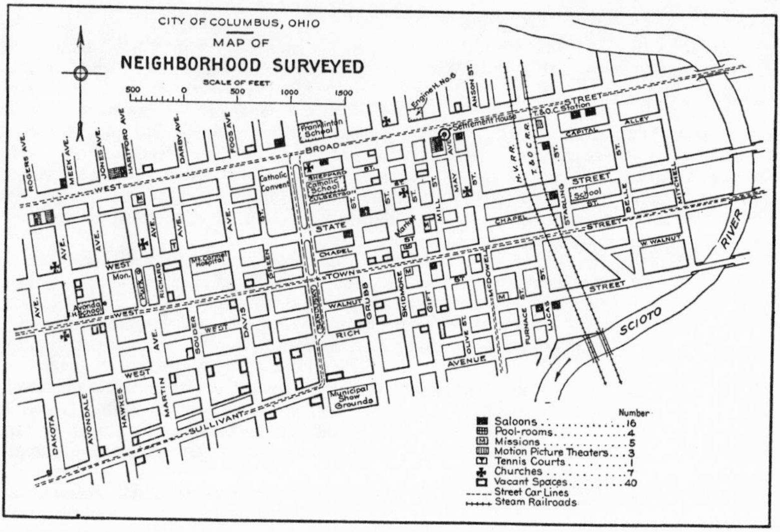

Map VI

reach every home in this district, but frequently the house was empty when the investigator called, and although second visits were made in most cases, still many households were thus unavoidably omitted. In the second place a study was made of all the neighborhood institutions—churches, schools, industries, and of all the forms of commercialized recreation. And lastly, special interviews were held with about twenty of the oldest residents of the district in order to obtain data concerning the history, leading changes, and dominant forces in the neighborhood.

The neighborhood that we are about to describe is located in the "flats" lying immediately west of the central part of the city. As indicated on Map VI, the region in question is bounded on three sides by a loop of the Scioto River. It comprises a low flood plane stretching west in triangular shape for about three miles to the Hilltop district. The eastern end of the district, or apex of the triangle, is less than a quarter of a mile in width, while the western base is about two miles wide. This district has been subject to periodic floods, occurring, according to reports of the oldest inhabitants, about every fifteen years. The most serious of these floods, in the memory of the oldest residents, took place in the spring of 1913 when the entire eastern half of the district was for a few days covered by water from six to ten feet in depth.

This neighborhood comprises one of the oldest sections of the city of Columbus. The central part of it was originally known as the village of Franklinton; the old county court building was located at the corner of Sandusky and Broad streets, the present site of the Franklinton School. Sullivant Avenue, the southern boundary line of the neighborhood, is named after Lucas Sullivant, the original owner of the "bottoms" lying west of the river. In the early days this district was so swampy and so undesirable for habitation that Mr. Sullivant gave lots to settlers to induce them to come and reside there. Hence Gift Street got the name it still retains.

The neighborhood was originally inhabited by "plain working people." Broad Street was the main thoroughfare and, in the opinion of many of the old timers, did a much more flourishing business twenty years ago than it does at present. The eastern section of the neighborhood, lying immediately west of the river, was, in the early days, known as "Middletown" and was considered by the people living farther west as a "rough" section. The local differentiation has, however, faded away; only a few of the old settlers seem to be familiar with the implication of the early local distinction.

There is general consensus of opinion among the older settlers that the neighborhood made a rapid decline immediately following the flood of 1913. At that time many of the more prosperous families moved to other parts of the city, especially to the new addition opened up just then on the Hilltop. Real estate prices declined rapidly, dropping to one-third or one-half their previous values. This in turn brought about an influx of colored and poor white families, with the consequent further deterioration of the neighborhood.

The area surveyed includes eleven precincts, which in 1918 had a total registered electorate of 1,824.[1] The city's registered electorate for that year was 45,854, or approximately one-sixth of the estimated population of the city as a whole. Figuring on this basis the district covered by our survey has a total population of approximately 11,000. The one-thousand households visited had a total population of 4,176, which is considerably over one-third of the estimated population of the entire neighborhood. Table III gives the distribution of the population according to age and sex.

TABLE III

AGE AND SEX DISTRIBUTION OF POPULATION OF NEIGHBORHOOD IN COMPARISON WITH THAT OF CITY AS A WHOLE

Age	Male	Female	Total	Percentage in Each Group	
				Neighborhood	City*
Under 5	215	242	457	10.9	7.9
5–9	216	229	445	10.6	7.4
10–14	216	198	414	9.9	7.4
15–19	152	197	349	8.4	9.1
20–24	158	182	340	8.1	11.1
25–34	318	343	661	15.9	20.6
35–44	253	301	554	13.3	15.5
45 and over	467	418	885	21.2	20.8
Unknown	40	31	71	1.7	0.2
Total	2035	2141	4176	100	100

* *U.S. Census*, 1910.

A few interesting facts are revealed by this table. For instance the ratio of small children for the neighborhood is considerably higher, and the ratio of adults, in the most productive years of life, considerably lower than for the city as a whole. In this area the percentage of children under fifteen years of age is 31.4 as against 22.7 for the city as given in the 1910 Census. On the other hand, the percentage of adults in the age group 15–45 is only 45.7 for the

[1] *Thirteenth Census of United States*, III (1910), 399.

neighborhood in contrast to 56.3 for the city. Again the proportion of the sexes in the neighborhood is quite different from that given in the 1910 Census for the city as a whole. In the district surveyed there are but 95 males to every 100 females as against 101.5 males to every 100 females in Columbus, and 104.4 males to every 100 females for the state of Ohio.[1]

TABLE IV

PLACE OF BIRTH OF WHITE ADULTS 18 YEARS AND OVER

Place of Birth	Husband	Wife	Others		Total
			Male	Female	
Columbus	179	194	135	136	644
Elsewhere in Ohio	418	462	185	155	1,220
Elsewhere in U.S.	147	157	50	51	405
Germany	21	19	4	1	45
Italy	17	15	1	2	35
Ireland	11	13	2	....	26
Great Britain	11	7	1	4	23
Austria	7	7	4	1	19
Switzerland	4	3	....	1	8
Roumania	2	....	....	....	2
Canada	....	1	1	....	2
India	1	....	....	....	1
Australia	1	....	....	....	1
France	1	....	1	....	2
Unknown	34	31	36	25	126
Total	854	909	420	376	2,559

It is quite evident that this is predominantly an American section of the city; 26.5 per cent of the adults whose place of birth is known were born in Columbus, 76.6 in Ohio, and only 6.7 per cent were born in countries other than the United States. Of those born outside of the United States only 111, or 4.5 per cent of the total population, come from non-English-speaking countries and these represent six different nationalities. With the exception of a small Italian neighborhood lying north of the subway on Rogers Avenue, there is no nucleus of foreign born in the entire district.

[1] These figures show that the population of the neighborhood contains more than a normal distribution of the economically weaker age and sex groups. Economic forces tend to distribute a city's population according to the relative strength of families in the competitive process.

Of our one thousand families forty-three were colored. If these were segregated in a single section of the district the number would be of minor significance as it comprises such a small percentage of the total population. But on the contrary these colored families are scattered over a large part of the neighborhood. Table V presents a list of the streets on which they dwell.

TABLE V

LOCATION OF COLORED FAMILIES

Street	Number of Families	Street	Number of Families
Chapel	6	Mill	1
Capital	1	Rich	1
Cherry	2	State	1
Grubb	3	Scott	2
Jones	3	Sandusky	4
Lucas	2	Starling	5
McDowell	8	Town	1
McKinley	2	W. Broad	1

A glance at the map of the neighborhood (p. 487) will show that colored people are to be found on almost every street from the river as far west as Sandusky Street, and, north of Broad Street, as far west as the survey extended.

Most of the colored families have made their way into this district since the flood of 1913. Of the forty-three households reporting, only two have been in the neighborhood more than six years; thirty-two, or 74.4 per cent, have been in the neighborhood less than three years; and nineteen, or 44.2 per cent, have been in the neighborhood less than one year. Most of these colored people are recent arrivals from the south, only nine of the heads of households were born in Ohio, eight came from Virginia, six from Georgia, four from Kentucky, three from Alabama, and the remaining thirteen from various other states throughout the Union.[1]

[1] My reason for discussing the colored family in detail is to emphasize its significance from the standpoint of neighborhood disintegration and decline. There is probably no more valid criterion of the disappearance of neighborhood sentiment in any locality inhabited by American people than to find colored families dispersed here and there among the white families. Where any degree of neighborhood consciousness exists social pressure invariably keeps the colored family out; but in the absence of local sentiment, the advent of the negro drives the more enterprising white folk to look for new quarters.

VI. MOBILITY OF NEIGHBORHOOD[1]

We have already discussed the question of mobility with reference to its more general aspects from the standpoint of the city as a whole. According to our general test of mobility, namely the percentage of the 1917 electors who failed to re-register in their

TABLE VI

HOME OWNERSHIP BY STREETS

Street	Owner	Renter	Percentage of Owners
Eastern section	102	367	21.8
Belle	3	19	13.6
Starling	2	15	11.7
McDowell	12	37	24.4
May	3	31	8.8
Mill	3	17	15.0
Gift	6	35	15.3
Broad	7	21	25.0
Capital	0	11	00.0
State	32	84	27.5
Chapel	12	32	27.2
Town	15	45	25.0
Walnut	7	22	24.0
Western section	138	226	38.0
Skidmore	20	30	40.0
Grubb	11	28	28.2
Sandusky	18	39	31.5
Davis	7	13	35.0
Souder	8	9	47.0
Richard	10	28	26.3
Martin	14	12	53.8
Hawkes	13	12	52.0
Avondale	8	9	49.0
Rich	15	35	30.0
Sullivant	14	11	56.0
Total	240	593	28.8

respective precincts in 1918, the eastern end of the neighborhood under consideration comprises one of the most mobile sections of the city. The two precincts which occupy the territory between the railroad tracks and the river lost almost two-thirds of their registered voters during the short period of one year. However, the neighborhood increases in stability the farther west one goes.

[1] The reader is referred to Map III (*Amer. Jour. of Sociol.*, XXVII [September, 1921], 163) for a general comparison of the mobility of this neighborhood with that of other sections of the city.

The precincts lying west of the railroad tracks, with one exception, have a re-registration of electors of over 50 per cent. This sectional difference in mobility is further emphasized by the difference in the percentage of home ownership for the two divisions of the neighborhood. For instance only 21.8 per cent of the homes between Skidmore Street and the river are owned by their present occupants, as against 38.1 per cent for the region lying immediately west of Skidmore Street. Table VI indicates the varying percentages of home ownership, by streets, for the two divisions of the neighborhood.

With respect to change of residence, Table VII gives the length of time each family has lived in its present home, in the

TABLE VII

COMPARATIVE MOBILITY OF TWO CITY NEIGHBORHOODS

Years	Columbus						Seattle*			
	House		Neighborhood		City		House		Neighborhood	
	No.	Percentage	No.	Percentage	No.	Percentage	No.	Percentage	No.	Percentage
0– 1.....	237	23.7	146	14.6	51	5.1	897	35.9	477	23.4
1– 2.....	158	15.8	99	9.9	33	3.3	447	17.9	311	15.3
2– 3.....	106	10.6	88	8.8	47	4.7	269	10.8	228	11.4
3– 4.....	102	10.2	89	8.9	41	4.1	155	6.2	135	6.6
4– 5.....	46	4.6	40	4.0	25	2.5	86	3.4	92	4.5
5– 6.....	44	4.4	46	4.6	30	3.0	92	3.7	101	4.9
6– 7.....	53	5.3	52	5.2	31	3.1	75	3.1	79	3.9
7– 8.....	15	1.5	28	2.8	23	2.3	78	3.1	94	4.6
8– 9.....	16	1.6	28	2.8	22	2.2	73	2.9	76	3.7
9–10.....	17	1.7	17.	1.7	14	1.4	45	1.8	67	3.4
10–15.....	84	8.4	104	10.4	106	10.6	200	8.0	235	11.5
15–20.....	37	3.7	82	8.2	115	11.5	53	2.1	88	4.3
20 and over	85	8.5	181	18.1	462	46.2	28	1.1	52	2.5
Totals...	1,000	100	1,000	100	1,000	100	2,498	100	2,035	100

* The neighborhood studied comprises about a square mile lying immediately adjacent to the campus of the University of Washington. It is a neighborhood of home owners of the middle economic classes. Fraternities and lodging houses were not included in this survey. The data were collected by the local Y.M.C.A. as part of the Interchurch World Survey in the winter of 1920.

neighborhood, and in the city, and compares the result with that of a similar study made of a neighborhood in a higher economic area in the city of Seattle, Washington.

It is apparent that the mobility of both of these neighborhoods is very high indeed. However, our broken-down neighborhood in

Columbus is even less mobile than the higher economic neighborhood of Seattle. In the former 60.3 per cent of the families were occupants of their homes for less than four years, and 42.2 per cent residents of the neighborhood less than four years, while in the latter neighborhood 70.8 per cent of the families have lived less than four years in their present homes and 56.5 per cent less than four years in the neighborhood.

Although the Columbus neighborhood has a large fringe of mobile families, still it also has a considerable stable nucleus. Over 18 per cent of the one thousand families visited have been residents of the neighborhood for twenty years or more, and of these families, 8.5 per cent have lived in their present homes throughout this period. This stable group forms the backbone of the neighborhood. Practically all of these householders are home-owners, and many of them are marooned superior families who are held in the neighborhood on account of property ties.

The data for Seattle are not comparable in this respect, owing to the fact that the district surveyed is relatively new. Most of the present homes have been erected during the past fifteen years. The high mobility, however, during the last five years is not entirely due to the erection of new dwellings, inasmuch as the older settled sections of the district show almost as high a mobility as the newer streets.

Unfortunately we have no information concerning the length of time the Seattle families have been residents of the city. It is interesting to note, however, that considerably over half, 57.7 per cent, of the male heads of households in our Columbus neighborhood have been residents of the city for fifteen years or more. It is quite evident, therefore, that the changes of residence among this economic class of the Columbus population are intra-community or intra-neighborhood rather than from one community to another.[1]

Change of family residence, however, does not tell the whole story concerning the mobility of the population of our Columbus

[1] Elsa G. Herzfeld found from a study of a group of tenement-house families in New York "that the average length of residence is about a year and a half," and that many of the moves are from "house to house in the same block."—*Family Monographs* (1905), p. 48.

neighborhood. It is also necessary to take into account the number of detached or floating persons who live as boarders or lodgers in the neighborhood. Our house-to-house canvass shows that there are 417 such persons, 236 males and 181 females, scattered among 267 of the 1,000 homes visited. This floating element is to be found for the most part in the eastern end of the district where the leading factories are located. Starling Street especially, due to its proximity to the railroad and the Godman Shoe Factory has become a center for boarding and lodging houses.

The relatively high physical mobility of the population of this neighborhood is somewhat counteracted by the lack of adequate means for communication. As was indicated elsewhere in this study mobility depends upon many factors other than the mere change of residence.[1] Time and means for getting about are also important considerations. Thus people living in the lower economic areas may have a high degree of mobility, so far as change of residence is concerned, and still be very much more dependent upon their neighborhood institutions than are the home-owners of the more stable and economically superior residential districts. The telephone, the automobile, and the business contacts give to the latter an independence of neighborhood organizations which the former do not possess. For this reason we have attempted to ascertain the facilities at the disposal of the people within this neighborhood for secondary means of communication.

Only 77 or 7.7 per cent of the 1,000 householders interviewed reported the ownership of an automobile.[2] And practically all of these machines are owned by families living on or west of Sandusky Street. In regard to the possession of telephones, 289 or 29.8 per cent of the households had this means of communication. This number of telephones may seem rather high, considering the low economic status of the neighborhood, but, as will be shown

[1] Cf. *Amer. Jour. of Sociol.*, XXVII (September, 1921), 167.

[2] The total number of persons in the 1,000 households was 4,176; this leaves one machine for every 56.8 inhabitants. According to the Goodrich Rubber Company report, there was, in 1919, one motor-vehicle for every 10.4 inhabitants in the state of Ohio; and one for every 14.2 inhabitants in the United States. Cf. J. Phelan, *Readings in Rural Sociology* (1920), p. 256.

later, the neighborhood is not a homogeneous economic unit. On the contrary it represents a mixture of families with respectable incomes living side by side with families who are in the utmost poverty.

If is difficult to measure the degree of dependence of this population upon its neighborhood institutions. The proximity of the region to the heart of the city makes the uptown institutions easily accessible to those with the means and desire to attend. That the different age and sex groups vary considerably in the degree to which they patronize the uptown institutions and places of amusement is shown by the facts brought to light in our study of the neighborhood churches and commercialized forms of recreation. Small children, mothers, and the older men are almost entirely dependent upon the neighborhood for their social and recreational life.

VII. ECONOMIC STATUS AND OCCUPATIONAL LIFE

The neighborhood surveyed falls in Wards 9 and 10; these two wards, it will be recalled, comprise the lowest economic area in the city. Ward 9, which includes the eastern end of the neighborhood, represents the lowest economic rating of all the wards in the city, having an average per-elector household-furniture appraisal, in 1917, of only $34.11. Ward 10, in which the major part of the neighborhood is located, has the second lowest rating with an average household furniture listing of $54.66.

Another index to the comparative economic status of different sections of a city is the average monthly rentals paid per dwelling. Unfortunately we have no data at hand to enable us to compare rentals of this neighborhood with those of other regions in the city. However, the facts revealed in Table VIII will convince the reader of the very low rental level of the territory surveyed.

Of the 656 rented homes concerning which we have information both as to rent and number of rooms, only 9, or 1.4 per cent, rent for more than $20 per month, while 524, or 79.9 per cent, rent for $15 or less. The average monthly rent per dwelling is $13.90 while the average number of rooms is five.

Table IX gives a classification of the occupations of the male heads of households.

The most striking feature brought to light by this somewhat detailed enumeration of employments is the industrial character of the neighborhood. This is a region where the soft collar and duck overalls predominate. Professional and business men form but a very small percentage of the heads of households. In this respect the neighborhood differs widely from the higher economic areas of the city. This fact is demonstrated by the lists (Table X, p. 499) of occupations of heads of households taken in order from two streets in other sections of the city.

TABLE VIII

RENTS PER MONTH IN RELATION TO SIZE OF DWELLING*

Rents per month	No. of Households Occupying Each Specified Number of Rooms										Total
	1	2	3	4	5	6	7	8	9	10	
Under $5	1	3	2	1	....	....	....	....	....	....	7
$ 5–$ 6	....	2	5	2	....	....	....	....	....	....	9
$ 6–$ 7	....	2	14	6	1	1	....	....	1	....	25
$ 7–$ 8	....	....	14	24	6	....	....	....	....	....	44
$ 8–$ 9	....	....	7	19	10	4	....	1	....	....	41
$ 9–$10	....	....	9	64	44	14	....	....	....	....	131
$10–$11	....	....	1	20	20	5	....	....	....	....	46
$11–$12	....	....	....	21	53	24	2	....	....	....	100
$12–$13	....	....	....	11	18	7	....	1	....	....	37
$13–$14	....	....	2	3	10	15	2	....	....	....	32
$14–$15	....	....	....	2	21	25	2	1	1	....	52
$15–$16	....	....	....	5	5	27	2	1	1	....	41
$16–$17	....	....	....	2	5	8	1	1	....	....	17
$17–$18	....	....	....	1	8	21	3	2	....	....	35
$18–$19	....	....	....	....	1	4	1	....	1	....	7
$19–$20	....	....	....	....	1	14	5	2	1	....	23
$20 and over	....	....	....	....	....	4	1	2	1	1	9
Total	1	7	54	181	203	173	19	11	6	1	656

* It must be kept in mind, however, that these figures represent conditions in May, 1919, before the general rise of rents in Columbus.

Although the west side neighborhood is primarily a workingman's district, still it by no means represents a uniform standard of living. Many of the heads of households, such as skilled laborers, railroad conductors, etc., belong to the higher income groups and could easily afford to live in one of the superior economic areas of the city. Proximity to work doubtless accounts for their residence here.[1] But on the other hand, the large number of different forms

[1] Fifty-two per cent of the adult male workers in our one thousand households walk to and from their work.

TABLE IX

OCCUPATIONS OF MALE HEADS OF HOUSEHOLDS

Working for Self	No.	Working for Others—Railroads	No.
Barber	2	Baggage man	3
Blacksmith	3	Blacksmith	3
Baker	1	Brakeman	11
Butcher	5	Boilermaker	5
Carpenter	2	Car inspector	3
Contractor	5	Clerk	7
Grocer	4	Conductor	16
Junkman	1	Engineer	11
Lawyer	1	Expressman	1
Paper hanger	4	Fireman	3
Painter	5	Foreman	4
Peddler	2	Freight man	2
Plasterer	2	Hostler	2
Repair man	1	Laborer	33
Real estate	3	Lineman	2
Saloon keeper	4	Machinist	14
Small business	8	Night watchman	2
Shoemaker	1	Railroader	17
Taxi driver	1	Repair man	2
Tailor	1	Switchman	2
Tinsmith	2	Transfer man	1
		Train caller	1
Total	58	Total	145

Working for Others—General	No.	Working for Others—General	No.	Working for Others—General	No.
Actor	1	Dyer	1	Painter	9
Bartender	8	Electrician	7	Paper hanger	3
Barber	4	Engineer	30	Penitentiary guard	3
Boiler maker	3	Fireman	11	Plumber	8
Blacksmith	3	Foreman	27	Policeman	9
Buffer	5	Furnace man	5	Printer	1
Butcher	6	Hotel clerk	4	Shipping clerk	7
Bookbinder	6	Insur. salesman	3	Soldier	4
Bookkeeper	1	Inspector	4	Salesman	14
Bank teller	1	Ice man	12	Shoemaker	25
Carpenter	21	Janitor	4	St.-car motorman	11
Clerk	35	Laborer	14	Solderer	3
Cabinet-maker	2	Lineman	4	Steel worker	21
Candy maker	2	Laundry man	2	Tinsmith	1
Cook	2	Lamp maker	1	Tailor	2
Collector	4	Meter reader	4	Taxi driver	1
Cooper	3	Machinist	31	Truck driver	30
Chauffeur	5	Molder	12	Undertaker	1
Chemist	2	Marble worker	1	Window trimmer	1
Decorator	2	Mail carrier	4	Retired	10
Detective	1	Mason	5	Unknown	48
Doctor	2	Meat packer	6		
Druggist	1	Night watchman	7	Total	631

of employment represented here indicate that this neighborhood is not a collectivity of workers grouped around some dominant industry such as we find in the neighborhood of the South Columbus Steel Works or in the stockyard district of Chicago.

Of the various industries represented in the neighborhood the railroads employ the largest number of the heads of households.

TABLE X

Street A, Ward 15 Occupation	No.	Street B, Ward 16 Occupation	No.
Building contractor	2	Attorney	3
Business man	10	Automobile dealer	3
Engineer	3	Building contractor	1
Lawyer	1	Clerk	4
Manufacturer	1	Conductor, steam R.R.	3
Newspaper editor	1	Electrical engineer	1
Night chief of police	1	Manufacturer	2
Physician	2	Real estate dealer	1
Restaurant proprietor	1	Retired	1
Traveling salesman	7	Superintendent R.R.	1
University professor	4	Traveling salesman	4
		University professor	1
		Wholesale merchant	4

TABLE XI

Name of Industry	No. of Employees			Percentage Resident in Neighborhood
	Total	Male	Female	
Godman Shoe Co.	550	230	220	25.0
Crystal Ice Co.	135	130	5	90.0
Doddington Lumber Co.	101	100	1	25.0

Our survey shows that 145 of the leading male breadwinners are engaged in some form or other of railroad employment. The Godman Shoe Factory comes second employing 30, and the Crystal Ice Company next, furnishing work to only 12 heads of households.

A survey of the main industries of the neighborhood, all of which are located in the northeastern end between the river and McDowell Street, gives the information presented in Table XI, with respect to the number of employees and the percentage of them residing within the neighborhood.

In regard to unemployment we succeeded in obtaining information concerning 865 male heads of households. Of this number 331, or 41.1 per cent, reported being off work for a period of seven days or more during the first three months of the present year (1919); and 110, or 13.6 per cent, reported being idle in this same period thirty days or more. Of the causes given for unemployment 26.7 per cent reported sickness, 35.1 per cent reported lack of work, and the remaining number, various other causes such as visiting, etc.

Our house-to-house canvass shows that 113 mothers work outside the home for remuneration. These are distributed among 25 different types of employment, day work and the shoe factory claiming the largest percentages.

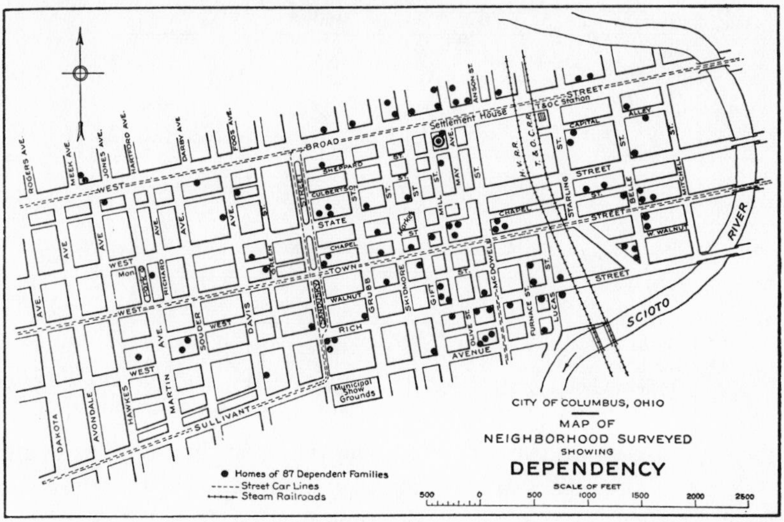

Map VII

The 87 official relief cases, the distribution of which is marked on our neighborhood map, do not give an accurate conception of the extent of poverty within the district. They merely indicate the number of families within the neighborhood who were actually obtaining relief from official sources at the time of our investigation. Had we taken the cases for a three-year period instead of one, the spots on the map would have given the appearance of almost solid black. Of course but a small percentage of the families below the poverty line actually come to the attention of the relief agencies of the city. My personal impression is, from reading over the notes on the one thousand schedules taken, that a large percentage of the families are in economic distress.

VIII. THE HOME AND DOMESTIC LIFE

Over 70 per cent of the houses of this district are single or duplex dwellings. Outside of Broad and State streets there are relatively few apartment houses. The buildings, in general, are

TABLE XII

ARTIFICIAL LIGHTING OF DWELLINGS

Means of Artificial Lighting	No. of Households Reporting	Percentage
Gas	794	79.4
Electricity	92	9.2
Oil lamps	99	9.9
Unknown	15	1.5
Total	1,000	100

TABLE XIII

HOUSEHOLD CONVENIENCES

Conveniences	No. of Homes	Percentage
Bath	407	40.7
Ice box	716	71.6
Toilet in house	435	43.5

placed close up to the streets leaving no room in front for lawns or grass. The blocks are laid out in such a way that there are few lanes or alleys, and most of the buildings on Broad Street have their entrances facing the side streets. The several alleys of the neighborhood, Capital, Chapel, etc., are dignified by the appellation "streets" and are used as such, having dwellings on both sides, although not more than thirty feet wide.

As one might expect, considering the low rentals charged, the houses of this district are, for the most part, obsolete. Tables XII and XIII give the results of our house-to-house canvass in this regard.

In regard to lighting it is interesting to note that there are more households using coal-oil lamps than there are using electricity. Gas, however, is the predominant method of lighting; almost 80 per cent of the dwellings use no other means of artificial illumination. Further, it will be observed that over 50 per cent of the homes are without baths or inside toilets. The absence of the ice box[1] in 29 per cent of the homes is also a point of significance for the public health authorities.

Table XIV shows the number of rooms per dwelling in relation to the number of occupants.

TABLE XIV

ROOMS PER DWELLING IN RELATION TO SIZE OF HOUSEHOLD

No. of Persons in Household	No. Using Specified Number of Rooms												Total
	1	2	3	4	5	6	7	8	9	10	11	Unknown	
1	2	3	2	3	2	1	1	1	....	1	....	5	21
2	....	3	27	53	63	38	7	7	3	1	....	10	212
3	....	1	11	42	70	44	18	10	....	....	1	6	203
4	....	....	7	39	42	52	10	13	5	1	1	1	171
5	....	....	9	34	46	47	9	8	2	2	....	1	158
6	....	2	3	16	31	27	4	6	3	3	....	......	95
7	....	....	1	16	24	30	8	7	3	....	....	......	89
8	....	....	2	3	5	11	3	2	1	1	....	......	28
9	....	....	....	2	5	3	....	....	....	1	..	......	11
10	....	....	....	1	....	2	....	1	....	1	....	......	5
11	....	....	....	....	1	1	....	....	....	....	....	......	2
12	....	....	....	....	1	3	....	....	....	....	1	......	5
Total	2	9	62	209	290	259	60	55	17	11	3	23	1,000

Unlike most industrial regions in large cities this neighborhood shows, at the date of survey, very little overcrowding in housing conditions. Of the households concerning which we have complete information, the average number of persons per room is 1.3. A significant fact brought out in the table is the large number of households of three or less members occupying dwellings of five rooms or more. There are 268 of these. But on the other hand 52 families, comprising 397 persons, are living in dwellings having less than two rooms for every three persons, which, according to housing standards, implies overcrowded conditions. And, as might be

[1] It is an interesting observation that the question in the schedule concerning the presence or absence of the ice box was the only one which consistently gave offense.

surmised, these dwellings are, for the most part, located along the alleys in the eastern section of the neighborhood.

Of the one thousand families visited 295 reported owning their own homes. In other words about 29 per cent of the homes of the entire district are occupied by their present owners. Unfortunately we do not possess the facts in regard to home-ownership for the city as a whole, consequently we cannot compare this neighborhood with other sections of the city. The percentage of home-ownership found here, however, is considerably higher than that of many of the big cities of the country where the apartment house abounds. For instance in Baltimore the ratio of home-ownership is 27.9 per cent, in Chicago 25.1 per cent, in Boston, 18.9, in New York 12.1, and in the crowded boroughs of Manhattan and the Bronx only 5.9 per cent.[1]

Although kinship does not any longer play the rôle that it once did in the organization of local life, nevertheless, it is still a factor in neighborhood selection within the city. Of the 1,000 households studied, 646 reported having one or more related families residing within the city of Columbus, and 476 households claimed kinship to one or more families living within the confines of the immediate neighborhood. These facts indicate that the bond of kinship continues to influence the territorial groupings of people within the city. This is especially true with respect to the lower economic areas. Mutual aid has almost ceased to be a factor in the fragmentary and casual relations between neighbors in the city environment. What direct co-operation remains, outside of the purposive organizations such as the trade unions and fraternal societies, is confined to the members of the family or kinship group.[2] This fact may partially explain the relatively high

[1] Munro, *Government of American Cities*, p. 48.

[2] I am aware that this statement does not correspond with the usual findings of social workers concerning the extent of mutual aid among tenement families. For instance Dr. Devine is quoted as saying "It is a question whether the unmeasured but certainly large amount of neighborly assistance given in the tenement houses of the city, precisely as in a New England village or in a frontier settlement, does not rank first of all among the means for the alleviation of the distressed."—Rev. John A. Ryan, Commencement Address to a graduating class in New York School of Social Work, 1920. For similar findings compare Elsa G. Herzfeld, *op. cit.*, pp. 33–34.

percentage of kinship found in this comparatively low economic region of the city. A very small percentage of the heads of households belong to the trade unions or voluntary societies of any sort, consequently there is greater need for reliance upon relatives in times of need.

The family group is now taken by welfare organizations as the unit for case-work. It is therefore important to know the salient facts about the family life of any region where social reconstruction is contemplated.

TABLE XV

AGE DISTRIBUTION OF MALE HEADS OF HOUSEHOLDS

Age in Years	Percentage of Heads of Households in Each Age Group	
	Neighborhood	Columbus
Under 25 years	3.9	6.2
25–44	50.8	57.2
45 and over	45.3	36.6

As was indicated by Table III (p. 489 of this article), and is further brought out here, the age distribution of the population within the neighborhood differs considerably from that of the city as a whole. The neighborhood has a distinctly lower percentage of people in the prime of life, and a considerably higher ratio of children and people over forty-five years of age. This condition is partially explained by the fact that a number of young men were still in military service when the survey was made. It may also be true, however, that during the more productive years of life many people are able to afford residence in the more desirable sections of the city, but, as their productive capacity declines with age, they are forced to retire to the lower rental areas.

Children per family.—Table XVI indicates the number of children per family under eighteen years of age residing at home at the time the survey was made.

Among our families, however, there was little evidence to show that mutual aid extended beyond the kinship group. There were of course occasional spots in the district where neighbors exchanged services but such cases seemed to be exceptional.

This table shows that about 25 per cent of the families reporting are without children living at home; that the average number of children per family is only 1.9, which of course is very low. The average is brought down, however, by the high percentage of households having no children at all. On the other hand there are 106 households where there are five or more children living at home. These large families are found, as a rule, in the broken-down streets and alleys of the neighborhood.

TABLE XVI

CHILDREN PER HOUSEHOLD, 18 YEARS AND UNDER

Children per Household	Households Reporting Each Specified Number of Children	
	No.	Percentage
None	249	24.9
1	219	21.9
2	192	19.2
3	138	13.8
4	96	9.6
5	76	7.6
6	13	1.3
7	8	.8
8	4	.4
9	2	.2
10	3	.3
Total	1,000	100

The broken family.—By the "broken family" we mean family groups where either or both parents, for some reason or other, are absent from home. Unfortunately, owing to the delicate nature of family problems, it was impossible to ascertain whether the parent's absence was due to death, divorce, desertion, or some other cause. Temporary absence, however, is not recorded in Table XVII.

It will be observed from this table that 15.6 per cent of the households may, according to our definition, be classified as broken families. Twenty-six households are listed as non-family groups; these comprise groups of non-relatives or at least distant relatives, living together in household association.

The unwholesome family.—As we have already indicated,[1] every normal individual possesses four general types of desires, namely, the desire for safety or security, the desire for recognition or social status, the desire for new experiences or stimulations, and the desire for mastery or power. If any one of these general desires is not getting adequate expression in the social environment the individual or group concerned tends to show signs of restlessness and discontentment, which may finally end in disorderliness or some other form of emotional disturbance. Whenever we find such dissatisfaction and maldirection of attention on the part of members of a

TABLE XVII

PARENTAL STATUS OF HEADS OF HOUSEHOLDS

Parental Status	No. of Households Reporting	Percentage
Both parents	818	81.8
One parent—father	20	2.0
One parent—mother	120	12.0
Neither parent present	16	1.6
Non-family groups	26	2.6
Total	1,000	100

family group, we call that group an "unwholesome family." Such families may not come under the supervision of any organized social agency; nor is it necessary that they be in adverse economic conditions to show signs of degeneracy and social unwholesomeness. Slums have been characterized as "areas of lost souls and missions,"[2] areas where individuals and family groups are living in enforced intimacy with people whom they naturally shun and avoid; areas where there are no standards of decency or social conduct except those imposed by outside authority. In such an environment the individual has no status, there is no representative citizen, the human desires for recognition and security remain unsatisfied.[3]

[1] See *Amer. Jour. of Sociol.*, XXVII (September, 1921), 160.

[2] From a mimeographed circular issued by Division of Immigrant Heritages, Americanization Bureau, New York, January, 1919.

[3] Joseph Lee, referring to the disorganizing influence of the slum environment, writes (*Play in Education* [1919], p. 382): "The danger, often realized, is that the city dweller may have no neighbors, or at least no neighborhood—no group of any

There are many instances of unwholesome families to be found within this neighborhood; let us give a few typical examples.

Case A: This is a family composed of husband, wife, and four small children. They live in a four-roomed dwelling for which they pay $10 per month. The home contains none of the modern conveniences such as bath, ice box, or toilet facilities. It is also bereft of musical instruments of any sort, books, or magazines. The family does not even take a daily paper. The husband is a day laborer and during the early part of the year was off work on account of illness for four weeks. According to its own report the family occasionally attends the street mission but none of its members belong to any outside social group. In the informant's language, "We never visit no one." The visitor makes the note, "The little girl, E, has never gone to school although she is nine years of age and apparently bright."

Case B: This family is composed at present of just father and mother, the children are all grown up and away. The couple live in about the same conditions as family A. The home is devoid of conveniences and cultural marks of any description. The husband drinks. He visits saloons and his wife does fancy work all day. They are not on friendly terms with their neighbors who say, "They swear and drink too much." The old lady says, however, "They are jealous of us, they throw bricks at our windows; it's a rough district." Investigator's note: "The wife wears a huge sunbonnet, has a frightened, piping voice, crochets, tats, and does fancy work continuously; she has four yelping dogs and three cats penned up in the kitchen, evidently to protect her; she is a regular story-book type of woman."

Case C: In this family there are husband, wife, and four children, the eldest of whom is but eleven years of age. The family lives in a five-roomed frame dwelling which is obsolete in every respect. They have been in the neighborhood five years and in the city six. The wife and children occasionally attend the Church of Christ but, outside of this, they have no form of social life. The wife dislikes

---

sort in which he feels a membership—no immediate social atmosphere, no standard which holds him up and which he feels it his business to uphold. He easily becomes the man without a neighbor almost as maimed as the man without a country or the man without a home."

the neighborhood because, "There are too many niggers and dogs." With regard to her neighbors she remarks, "We leave each other alone." Investigator's note: "The woman told me that she lacked but one month of graduating from a southern Presbyterian college when she married. She seems satisfied with the slum life but told me how awfully poor they are; they can't even afford an evening paper."

Case D: This family has seven members, father, mother, and five children the eldest of whom is about eighteen. The family has been in the neighborhood just six months, having moved there from a country district. So far, it has not found itself in its new environment. The only recreational or social life reported by the family is an occasional attendance at the motion-picture show. The family has lost social status since coming to the city and is in a position to become disorganized. The mother said to the investigator, "We used to keep up in society, but just can't any more, my son could dance like they danced in the country but of course town dancing is more like society." They do not like the neighbors round about them because "they fight and beat each other."

These are but a few cases selected at random from a large number of a similar sort. They represent what we call "unwholesome families," that is to say, some of the dominant attitudes and values which are necessary to make life wholesome and thriving are missing. It should be part of the duty of the neighborhood social worker to get acquainted with all such families under his jurisdiction and help them to help themselves by discovering their wants and needs and then linking them up with the organization or social group with which the respective members most closely identify their personalities, thereby arousing a new interest and motive for living.

The marooned family.—It is quite as important for the social worker in a broken-down neighborhood to know his sources of aid as to be familiar with the pathological conditions with which he has to deal. For this reason we wish to call attention to the fact that there are many families in all parts of this neighborhood who are as competent and as intelligent citizens as are to be found in any other section of the city. Many of these families are long-time residents of this neighborhood, who on account of home-ownership or other local attachments have been compelled to remain here long after the surrounding area has become disintegrated and broken down. Such families usually have a desire to help rehabilitate their surroundings, but, realizing their individual helplessness, despair of any accomplishment. A few become rancorous and soured toward the region of their habitation and hold themselves aloof from any form of contact with the people round about. Their interests and associations are in other sections of the community, consequently they feel no dependence whatever upon their neighborhood institutions and have no interest in their welfare. The two following cases are typical examples of "marooned families."

Case A: This family consists of father, mother, and three grownup children. They own their home and have been living in the neighborhood for the past fifteen years. The father is an engineer, the daughter a stenographer, and one of the sons is a student at the university. The family is living in a section of the neighborhood that has fallen to pieces during the last few years. The mother informed the investigator: "This is a horrible place to live in but we can't leave on account of our property." Investigator's note: "This is a high type of family, not to be compared with the people round about."

Case B: This family is living in the eastern section of the neighborhood. They have been in their present home for thirty-nine years. The family is composed of a widowed mother, sixty years of age, and three grownup children, two sons and a daughter. The older boy is an automobile salesman, the younger one had not returned from the army on the date of visit. All members of the family belong to the Catholic church which they report attending regularly. They have a phone, piano, and over one hundred books in their library. The family is anxious to sell their home and get out of the neighborhood. They consider the people living round about as "nothing but trash." Investigator's note: "This is a nice old lady; she considers the neighborhood run down and refuses to have anything to do with the families around her except the K's."

THE NEIGHBORHOOD: A STUDY OF LOCAL LIFE IN THE CITY OF COLUMBUS, OHIO

R. D. McKENZIE
University of Washington

ABSTRACT

Religion and the church. Differences in religious and moral attitudes are potent elements in the determination of lines of association in this neighborhood. The Catholic church is a dominant force, but most of the Protestant churches are losing ground. Missions, representing the more mystical creeds, enlist the interest of a considerable element of the population. *Education and delinquency.* Part of this neighborhood has the lowest school-attendance rating of any section in the city. The children attending one of the schools in this section were rated by a psychologist as mentally two years below the children attending a school in a higher economic area of the city. Juvenile delinquency is slightly more prevalent in this neighborhood than in the city as a whole. *Neighborhood sentiment.* Positive sentiment for the neighborhood and surrounding neighbors is rarely expressed by resident family groups. Occasional streets, however, contain intimate neighborly groups of people who are happy in their physical and social surroundings.

IX. RELIGION AND THE CHURCH

Our chief interest in wishing to know the religious affiliations of the people of this neighborhood is to get some clue concerning the diversity of their voluntary associations. A study of any residential area within a city always reveals the great complexity of the associational life of its inhabitants. The crossings and recrossings of individual interests show that neighborhood association alone is not adequate to meet all the needs of human nature. Table XVIII gives in considerable detail the religious preference of the adults of this neighborhood as obtained from our house-to-house canvass. It includes all persons indicating religious preference, not merely church members or attendants.

It will be observed that there is a considerable range of difference in the religious preference of the people in this district. Approximately 32 per cent of all adults reporting, 38 per cent of the men and 26 per cent of the women, deny affiliation with any religious group. Of those indicating religious preference, 520, or 22.8 per cent, incline toward the Catholic faith, and, for the most part, are members of the Holy Family Church within the neighborhood. The remaining 1,317, or 87 per cent, indicate preference for one or other of the various Protestant sects listed in Table XVIII. It will be noted that a very considerable portion of those of Protestant faith belong to the more mystical and orthodox types of religious sects.

TABLE XVIII

RELIGIOUS AFFILIATION

	Male	Female	Total
No. reporting no church affiliation	488	363	851
No. reporting affiliation with Catholic churches	237	283	520
No. reporting affiliation with Protestant churches	575	742	1,317
Sectarian distribution of Protestants:			
Methodist	195	247	442
Baptist	73	90	163
Presbyterian	68	82	150
Lutheran	47	60	107
Church of Christ	36	65	101
Episcopal	37	49	86
United Brethren	34	38	72
Spiritualist	15	25	40
Congregational	10	10	20
Protestant Church	8	3	11
Seventh-Day Adventists	4	7	11
Holy Rollers	4	7	11
Christian Science	1	8	9
Salvation Army	2	6	8
Missions	41	45	86
Total number of persons reporting	1,300	1,388	2,688

The facts brought out in our religious census, together with the general attitudes expressed on religious questions, go to show that the people of this neighborhood constitute a peculiar mixture of intense religious enthusiasm combined with religious apathy or pronounced religious antagonism. In other words the apparent homogeneity of the population of this area, as revealed by the external physical and cultural conditions, is, for the most part, superficial. A study of the inner associational life of the people shows that there exist wide chasms of difference in social attitudes.

That religious bias is an important factor in determining lines of association and group life is indicated by the following expressions of typical attitudes: "We have our own Spiritualist friends and don't bother any one else." "I don't like this district, too

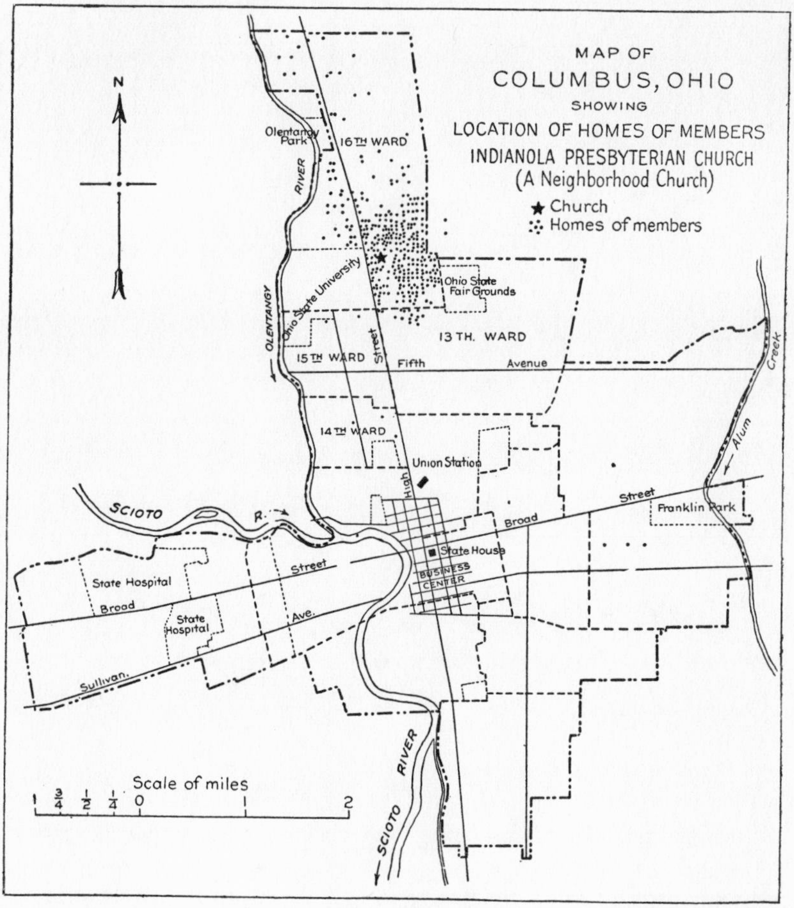

MAP VIII

many niggers and Holy Rollers." When asked concerning attendance at motion-picture shows, one woman replied, "Pictures are sending thousands straight to hell, dances are worse, I'm plain spoken." Another woman remarked, "I want to leave this neighborhood, I have Catholics on both sides of me." Such examples might be multiplied indefinitely, attention is drawn to them merely to illustrate the difficulties involved when attempting to bring

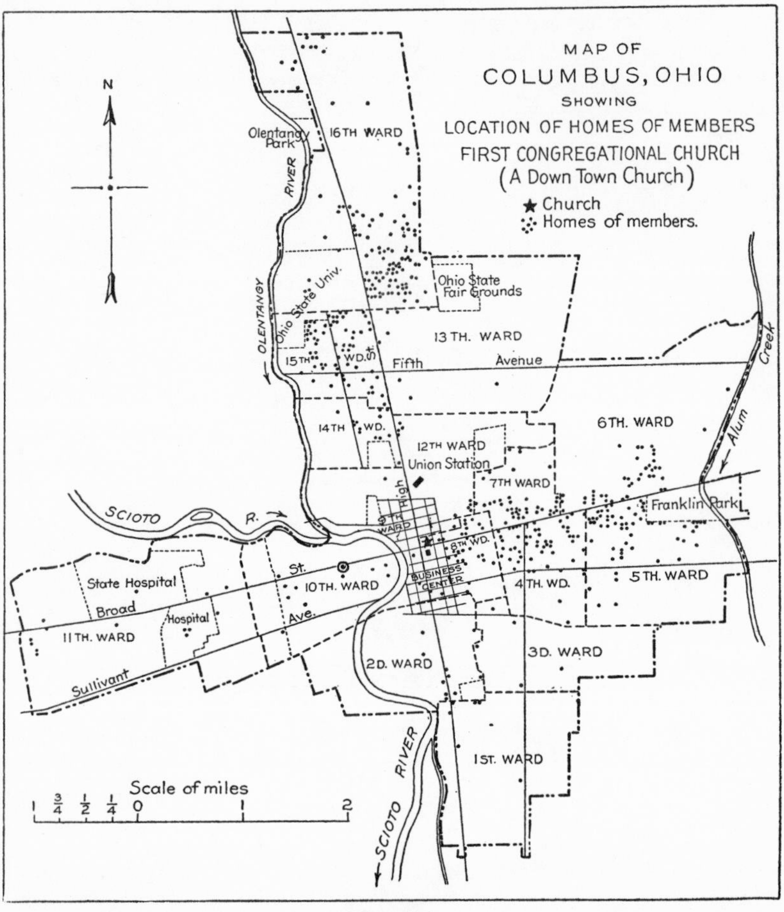

Map IX

individuals of different religious and moral attitudes into a common plane of association.[1]

City churches may be roughly grouped into two general classes: neighborhood churches and non-neighborhood churches. The

[1] "It is assumed, I suppose, that any idea or group of ideas, any belief or group of beliefs, may happen to be, or may become, a common interest, shared by a small or a large number of individuals. It may draw and hold them together in bonds of

former type selects its members largely on the basis of proximity, the latter type selects its members chiefly on the basis of individual preference or interest without respect to locality.

The distribution of a church's members determines the rôle which it may play as a neighborhood builder. It is difficult to focus attention on neighborhood affairs among a congregation that is widely distributed throughout the entire city. Maps VIII and IX illustrate the two types of churches referred to.

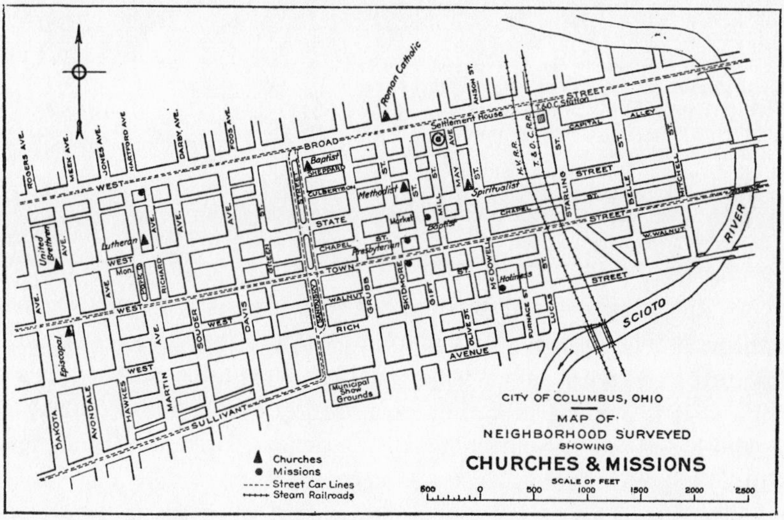

Map X

Within the district surveyed there are seven churches and five missions, the locations of which are marked on Map X. A summary of the leading facts concerning these religious institutions will give some indication of the rôle they play in the life of the neighborhood. In the first place it must be noted that the churches vary considerably in the extent to which they draw their member-

acquaintance, of association, even of co-operation. It thus may play a group-making rôle. Contradictory ideas or beliefs, therefore, may play a group-making rôle in a double sense. Each draws into association the individual minds that entertain it or find it attractive. Each also repels those minds to whom it is repugnant, and drives them toward the group which is being formed about the contradictory idea or belief. Contradictions among ideas and beliefs, then, it may be assumed, tend on the whole to sharpen the lines of demarkation between group and group."—Giddings: "Are Contradictions of Ideas and Beliefs Likely to Play an Important Group-making Rôle in the Future?" *Amer. Jour. of Sociol.*, 2XIII, 784.

ship from the neighborhood round about. For instance four of the churches report that over 90 per cent of their members live within walking distance of their respective places of worship; the fifth church reports that 50 per cent of its members live within walking distance, the sixth 35, and the seventh only 10 per cent. This information will help in the interpretation of the following facts.

TABLE XIX

SUMMARY OF LEADING FACTS WITH RESPECT TO THE CHURCHES

	Protestant Churches	Catholic Church
Total seating capacity of church auditoriums..........	2,250	800
Total membership (Communicants)...................	1,730	1,400
Total membership under 21 years of age, four Protestant churches reporting................................	283	700
Total average morning attendance, four Protestant churches reporting................................	390	1,250
Total average evening attendance, five Protestant churches reporting................................	623	....

In the area covered by our survey there is a population of approximately 11,000. Considering the fact that these religious institutions serve a much wider region than that covered by the survey, it is evident that they do not play a very important rôle in the life of the neighborhood. Of the four Protestant churches supplying information, 23.7 per cent of their members are less than twenty-one years of age, and 50 per cent of the members of the Catholic church fall below this age limit. Five of the six ministers of the Protestant churches reported having difficulty in maintaining the interest of the young people of their congregations, while Father Clarke of the Holy Family Church stated that he had no problem in this regard. Furthermore, the four Protestant churches giving information reported an average attendance of only 33.7 per cent of their members at the morning service and 44.6 per cent at the evening service.

In addition to the churches just described, there are five missions in the neighborhood. It is interesting to note that these, like the saloons, are located in the eastern and northern sections of the district, that is, in the most disintegrated parts of the neighborhood. These missions were all visited by our investigator and information was obtained concerning the type of attendants, nature of teachings, and extent of their activities. They are all open on week nights, and report a total average nightly attendance of 115, and a total average Sunday attendance of 320 people. In their preaching they emphasize Holiness, Gift of Tongues, Sanctification, etc. An interesting fact about these organizations is that most of them are products of the distant past, some of them dating back half a century or more. They are real, live, social organisms which owe their existence to the fact that they satisfy real needs in the lives of a people whose normal human desires have been stifled or misdirected by an adverse social environment. The mission affords an opportunity for self-expression and status in another world to those who, in the competitive social process, have lost social security and recognition, which indeed is the explanation of the "lost soul."

Of the six Protestant churches in the district, five gave information concerning their Sunday-school activities. These reported a total average weekly attendance in adult classes of 114, in intermediate classes, 241, and in classes for children, 130. These figures become significant when we interpret them in the light of the wider group statistics. In the territory which they serve there are approximately 3,000 children under eighteen years of age, which implies that only one out of every nine children is enrolled in a Protestant Sunday school. These figures are somewhat temporized, however, by the fact that the one Catholic church in the district has an average attendance of 360 children in its Sunday morning classes.

The six Protestant churches report the following societies in connection with their church work: eight societies for women with a total membership of approximately 250, four of which are devoted to missionary enterprises; four organizations for men with a total membership of 97; four young people's societies with an approximate membership of 235; four societies for girls with a total membership of 110; and one boy scout organization with a membership of thirty. Most of these societies have meetings once or twice a month with occasional social functions of a more general character.

In the six churches referred to, there are nine parlors with a total seating capacity for approximately three hundred people. Two of the churches have pianos, one a stereopticon, one a gymnasium, two libraries, and four have kitchens. The recreational activities of the Catholic church are carried on under the direction of the parochial school and Father Clarke reports that a fully equipped gymnasium is now being constructed in the school building.

In reply to the question, "What additional equipment would the pastor like?" we received the following statements: (1) "Basketball equipment, bowling alley in basement, a pool table, and a trained social worker." (2) "A community house and playground in connection." (3) "A stereopticon and some good games." (4) "The best thing is to have some religious service every night in the week." (5) "A bulletin board, a movie lantern, above all we lack leadership." (6) One pastor considers that it is not the function of the church to engage in welfare work.

X. LEISURE-TIME ACTIVITIES

This district is by no means a unit so far as equipment of homes for leisure-time activities is concerned. With respect to the possession of musical instruments, books, magazines, and indoor games, a considerable number of the homes are furnished quite as well as those in the higher economic areas of the city. This is particularly true with reference to many of the homes west of Sandusky and south of Broad Street; and there are also homes scattered in other sections of the neighborhood where facilities for indoor leisure-time activities are by no means lacking. On the other hand, a large percentage of the homes of the entire neighborhood are pathetically bereft of any sort of equipment whatever for the fruitful expenditure of leisure time. For instance, many of the homes have little or no reading material other than the daily paper[1] and some families are either too poor or too ignorant to afford even that.

It will be noted that over 50 per cent of our one thousand families have in their homes no musical instrument whatever. On the other hand, 20 per cent of the homes contain pianos. This is merely further evidence of the heterogeneous character of the

[1] It is noteworthy that 76 per cent of the families reported taking as their daily paper the *Citizen*, an evening paper which features dramatic news and human interest stories. This paper's city circulation is quite large but not equal to that of its less dramatic competitor the *Columbus Despatch*.

population of this neighborhood. Poverty and sufficiency, viciousness and respectability, are to be found side by side in this area of the city.

It might be expected, owing to the relatively small part organized club life plays in the lives of the people of this district, that

TABLE XX

POSSESSION OF MUSICAL INSTRUMENTS

NAME OF MUSICAL INSTRUMENT	FAMILIES REPORTING EACH SPECIFIED KIND OF INSTRUMENT	
	No.	Percentage
No instrument	506	50.6
Piano	218	21.8
Organ	16	1.6
Phonograph	181	18.1
Piano and phonograph	58	5.8
Organ and phonograph	4	.4
Unknown	17	1.7
Total	1,000	100

social visiting would be the normal and customary way of spending leisure time. For this reason an attempt was made to ascertain to what extent social visiting was customary, either within, or without the neighborhood. For obvious reasons it was difficult to get accurate information on this point; consequently the following summary of facts is at best but an approximate statement of the truth.

TABLE XXI

EXTENT OF SOCIAL VISITING WITHIN AND WITHOUT THE NEIGHBORHOOD[1]

	No.	Percentage
Number of families reporting no visiting at all	235	23.5
Number reporting more visiting within than without neighborhood	506	50.6
Number reporting more visiting outside neighborhood	222	22.2
Number reporting equal amount of visiting within and without neighborhood	22	22.
Unknown	15	1.5
Total	1,000	100

[1] In our survey we defined social visiting as calling on a family in its home and not merely talking over the back fence. Neighborhood was defined as the area within walking distance of the home.

The astonishing thing about this table is the large number of families—23 per cent—that reported no visiting at all. The usual explanation was: "I have too much to do, have no time for visiting" or "I attend to my own business and let other folk attend to theirs."

It is apparent that social visiting is, to a large extent, becoming obsolete even among the poorer classes as a means of employing leisure time. This is doubtless due to the mobility and anonymity of modern city life where personal acquaintance and neighborhood association have largely become a thing of the past.[1] In contrast to this it is interesting to note the replies of the old-timers to the question, "What were the principal old-time forms of recreation in the neighborhood?" The following answers are typical: "Picnics, neighborhood dances, barn dances, fishing parties, friendly visiting, etc."

There are two leading amusement areas in the neighborhood where large numbers of the people, both young and old, gather every evening. These areas are the best lighted and gayest spots in the district. They can be easily recognized by even the casual visitor to the neighborhood as the local fountain heads of amusement. Both are located on Broad Street—one between May and Mill avenues, the other farther west on Broad between Hartford and Jones avenues. In the first area there are two saloons, each having a poolroom in the rear, a motion-picture theater, an air dome, a restaurant, a barber shop, and a shoe-shining parlor.

The three motion-picture theaters of the neighborhood are located in the two areas just referred to. One of these is really

[1] With the disintegration of the neighborhood a large element of any city's population is suffering from the lack of intimate associates. This is particularly true with reference to the mothers of small children. The disorganizing effect of loneliness has never been adequately analyzed. Graham Wallas says (*The Great Society* [1914], p. 350), "The fact . . . . that there is a Mean in our powers of forming acquaintance, that it is joy to know enough people and a weariness to know too many, affects not only the group-organization of the Great Industry, but also the life of the industrial worker during the now slowly lengthening interval between his work and his sleep. The young unmarried artisan, or shopman, or clerk generally lives either in a one-roomed lodging with a defect of intimate association or in a great boarding-house with an excess of it. Outside his factory or office, he may either know no one to speak to or have a hundred nodding acquaintances and no friend."

not a theater but an air dome and is closed during the winter months. Our investigator visited all three of these and had interviews with their managers. From the standpoint of sanitation and fire protection they were all reported as being in "fair" condition. The pictures shown were reported as being "thrilling, adventurous, daring"; nothing immoral or disorganizing was detected. According to the investigator's estimate of the age distribution of the audiences, 75 per cent in one, 65 per cent in the second, and 85 per cent in the third were under eighteen years of age. The audiences were, for the most part, made up of people

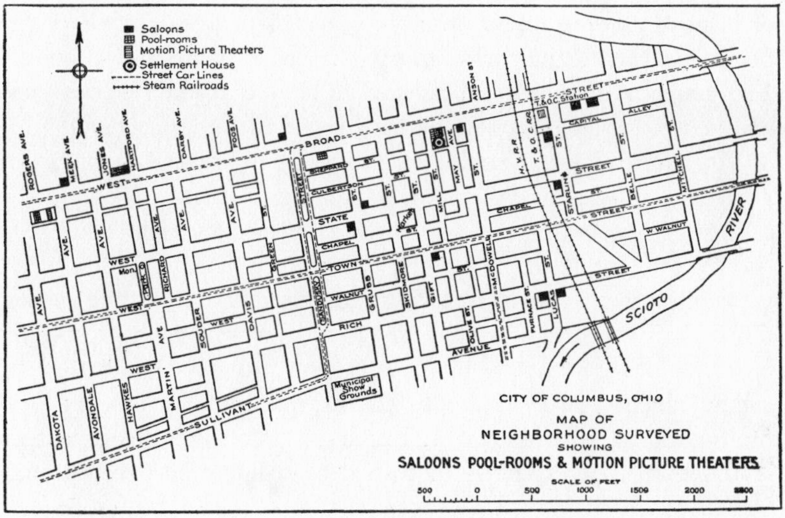

MAP XI

living within the immediate neighborhood, over 90 per cent of whom walked to the shows. The three theaters have a total seating capacity of 870, and an average daily attendance of about 800. In two of the theaters shows are held every evening with an additional matinee on Sunday. The third theater is open but four evenings of the week. Pictures are changed in all three theaters for each performance. A charge of ten cents for adults and of from six to ten cents for children is made.

It is very evident that the motion-picture show is the most popular form of amusement for the people of this neighborhood. The results of our house-to-house canvass show that, for the women and children at least, the moving picture is the predominant type of recreation. The comparatively high percentage of small children in attendance at the shows is explained by the fact that the youth of the neighborhood are drawn to the more attractive and, for them, easily accessible forms of amusement in the heart of the city, while the older men attend the saloons and many of the mothers remain at home.

There are eight poolrooms in the neighborhood, three of which are connected with saloons. They all happen to be located on Broad Street. The poolroom is primarily the social club for the young men. About 50 per cent of the patrons present on the dates of inspection were under twenty-one years of age. In all of the poolrooms the conduct was reported as being "orderly and quiet." The young men, in general, seemed to be well acquainted with one another and used the poolroom as a social meeting place.

As indicated on Map XI there are at present (August, 1919) seventeen saloons within the area surveyed. These saloons have all been inspected twice; once in May before the demise of John Barleycorn, and again in August, two months after prohibition had gone into effect. An interesting fact brought out in the second tour of investigation was that all the saloons were found to be still open and doing an active business in "soft" drinks, confectionery, cigars, lunches, etc. In reply to the question, "Does the proprietor intend to continue in business?" four of the seventeen stated that they expected to turn their saloons into restaurants. One proprietor said that he was making more money than formerly; the remainder indicated that they were awaiting the results of the fall elections and the effects of the advent of cold weather on their soft drink business. Sixteen of the seventeen saloons were furnished with card tables; approximately 75 per cent of which were in active use on the evenings of investigation.

There are three distinct types of saloons in this neighborhood, characterized by the form of service rendered and the class of patron served. In the first place there is the "social club" saloon which serves as the evening clubhouse for the older men of the neighborhood. Saloons of this type are to be found, for the most part, west of Gift Street; they are all well equipped with card tables and owe their existence largely to the fact that they are social meeting places for the older men of the neighborhood who are too tired after a day's work to go up town to the more dramatic but less sociable resorts on High and Front streets. Very few men under thirty years of age were found in these social-club saloons. Moreover the patrons seemed to be intimately acquainted with one another and spent their time in talking and playing "rummy" for the drinks. This type of saloon plays a very important part in the life of this particular class of people in the neighborhood. In fact the club life afforded by the saloon seems to be the only form of group association, outside the narrow circle of the home, in which the older males participate.

The second type of saloon is that which caters to the transient class of patrons. Saloons of this character are located on Broad Street, especially east of the subway where the chief industrial establishments of the neighborhood are situated. Such saloons do not encourage club life, and the patrons are, as a rule, strangers to one another who merely stop in for a drink and then depart.

The third and most questionable type of saloon is the "sporting-resort," used as a meeting place for young people who are attracted by this sort of life. The eastern section of the neighborhood contains several saloons of this character. The two saloons on Starling Street and the two on Lucas and Rich streets are the leading representatives of this class. They contain rear parlors of a somewhat questionable nature and are frequented by young men, "professional bums," who very probably do not live in the neighborhood but merely resort there periodically. Such rendezvous are a menace to the life of the neighborhood inasmuch as they attract the undesirable elements from the larger community and thus tend to disorganize the local area by driving out the more respectable families.[1]

[1] Nowhere is the individualizing force of the city environment more clearly revealed than in the individual selection of leisure-time activities. Commercialized forms of recreation are organized to cater to the special interests of the different age, sex, and cultural groups of the population. Thus in our neighborhood the older men prefer the informal sociability of the saloon club life; the young men are attracted by the more active forms of amusement offered by the poolroom, or by the sex attractions of the cabaret or cheap dance hall; the young women attend the up-town dance halls or the movies; the small children attend the movies, while the mothers have little or no recreational life save an occasional visit to the motion-picture theater or the club life afforded by the church.

Leisure-time activities of children.—Through the kind co-operation of the principals and teachers of the three public schools in the neighborhood, a census was taken in the early part of May, 1919, of the after-school activities of all the children in Grades III to VIII inclusive. On a Monday morning the children were instructed by their teachers to relate in writing just how they had spent their time after leaving school Friday afternoon until they went to bed

TABLE XXII

TYPES OF ACTIVITIES REPORTED BY 350 SCHOOL BOYS FOR A TWO-DAY PERIOD, MAY 23–24, 1919

Time	Playing Baseball	Roaming, Fishing, Swimming	Attending Picture Shows	Undesignated Play	Reading, Studying	Working			Going up Town
						Street Trades	Other Work for Pay	Helping Parents	
Fri. afternoon....	32.0	8.6	.8	16.0	6.9	10.6	12.3	33.1	5.1
Fri. evening......	16.8	7.4	20.0	13.0	30.8	1.4	4.4	15.4	4.6
Sat. morning.....	16.0	13.0	......	30.8	5.0	7.0	14.8	33.7	12.3
Sat. afternoon....	25.4	9.2	3.8	14.0	4.3	8.3	13.4	21.7	14.0
Sat. evening......	9.7	8.3	27.4	12.3	12.3	3.0	8.6	16.0	15.0

TABLE XXIII

TYPES OF ACTIVITIES REPORTED BY 375 SCHOOL GIRLS FOR A TWO-DAY PERIOD MAY 23–24, 1919

Time	Undesignated Play	Walking, Visiting, Picnics	Attending Picture Shows	Doing Nothing	Reading, Studying, Music	Working for Pay	Helping Parents	Going up Town
Fri. afternoon...	29.3	7.7	1.9	2.1	24.3	4.0	56.0	8.3
Fri. evening....	29.1	11.7	14.1	4.0	38.1	.8	32.3	2.4
Sat. morning....	12.3	5.1	7.5	.3	7.1	2.4	79.7	10.7
Sat. afternoon...	22.1	17.3	18.3	1.6	12.3	3.2	33.6	27.7
Sat. evening....	20.0	13.9	25.0	2.9	18.1	1.3	22.7	15.7

Saturday night. In Tables XXII–XXIII an attempt has been made to classify the recorded activities according to the specified time intervals.

Owing to the striking dissimilarity of the activities reported by the boys and the girls it was found necessary to make separate classifications. For instance social visiting and picnicing are popular activities with the girls while fishing and roaming are more attractive to the boys. In both tables the term "undesignated play" includes all sorts of general statements such as "After school I went home and played till supper time" or "I went out and played with the kids." It will be observed that a very considerable part of the play activities of both sexes is of this general, unorganized, and undirected nature. It simply means that the children are out in the streets and alleys chasing one another around as the occasion or impulse may direct. Play of this sort usually ends up in mischief or disorderliness, with the subsequent formation of predatory gangs. The favorite game among the boys is baseball. The girls, on the other hand, seem to have no outstanding form of play. The traditional attitude that a girl is supposed to work or mind the baby rather than waste her time in play is clearly exemplified by the facts revealed in these tables. The large percentage of girls who report "helping parents" shows that the main activity, after school hours, is doing housework. Working for pay, however, is much less common among the girls than among the boys, as over 20 per cent of the latter report "working for remuneration." The most popular form of evening amusement for both girls and boys is going to the movies. In this respect the percentages for both sexes are about equal. From 20 to 25 per cent of all the children report attending the motion-picture theater on both Friday and Saturday evenings. Another fact of interest in regard to these tables is the large number of both boys and girls who go up town on Saturday evening. Of the girls who thus reported 8 per cent gave no particular reason for their action, merely making such general statements as, "After supper I went up town" or "On Saturday night I went up town," or as one girl of fourteen put it, "On Saturday night I went up town for awhile and then I went to Olentangy Park and danced till ten o'clock." Two main factors are conducive to this going-up-town habit; first, the proximity of the neighborhood to the center of the city, and second, the individualism of the modern family which finds its extreme expression in such neighborhoods as this.

The school and recreation.—There are three public schools in the district, two elementary and one intermediate, having an aggregate daily attendance, in 1919, of 1,644 pupils. The two elementary schools, Fieser and Franklinton, which include Grades I to VI, draw all their pupils from the immediate neighborhood covered by our survey. The district of the Avondale intermediate school, however, extends considerably farther west; about two-thirds of the pupils attending come from the Hilltop or adjoining territory.

The Fieser School, located at the corner of State and Starling streets, is in the midst of the most broken-down area on the west side. It has an average daily attendance of approximately 450 children ranging in ages from six to twelve years. The building is old and very ill-adapted to the service which a school should perform in modern community life. It is heated by hot air and has no ventilation system other than the windows and doors. Moreover it contains no artificial lighting system of any sort. Not only is this a tremendous handicap to the general work of the day school but it makes it impossible to use the building at night for neighborhood meetings.

The Fieser School has a total play space of approximately 23,000 square feet which is divided by outbuildings into three different areas. Considering that there are about 450 pupils attending the school, this makes an average play space of about 50 square feet per child. Taking 145 square feet per child, the minimum amount of space agreed upon by experts as necessary for circle games, it is obvious that Fieser School falls far below this standard.

The Franklinton Elementary School, located at the corner of Broad and Sandusky streets, has an enrolment this year (1919) of 550 pupils. There is a total ground space at this school of approximately 10,000 square feet which is divided into two long, narrow strips, one about 18 feet wide used by the boys, the other 15 feet wide comprising the girls' playground. It is apparent that these strips are entirely inadequate for any sort of group games. They do not even afford room for slides, teeters, etc., nor is there space adequate for the playing of basket-ball. The school has no gymnasium; one room in the basement might be used for this purpose if it were properly floored and ventilated.

The Avondale Intermediate School, located on the corner of Avondale and Town streets, has an enrolment of about 600 pupils. It has a play space of approximately 40,000 square feet which gives considerably more room per child than is provided at the Franklinton School. There is no outdoor playground equipment but the principal expects to start basket-ball and indoor baseball soon. There is no gymnasium in the school.

In addition to the fact that the schools of the neighborhood afford but little opportunity for healthful play we must note that the district facilities for outdoor recreation are also much below the average for the city as a whole. The houses and apartments of the neighborhood, with very few exceptions, are built close up to the sidewalks leaving no lawn or play spaces. Further, the backyards

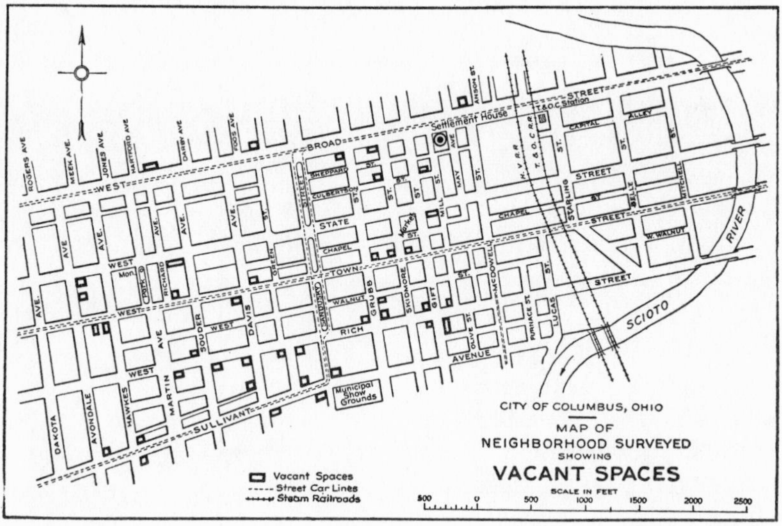

MAP XII

are small and, for the most part, filled up with old shacks and weeds making them inaccessible for play purposes. These statements apply particularly to the eastern half of the district, especially to the section between Grubb Street and the river.

On the accompanying map (XII) of the neighborhood we have shown all the available open spaces which are large enough for children's games. It will be noted that east of McDowell Street there is not a single vacant lot upon which the children may play, and it may also be said of this region that there is scarcely a single lawn or patch of grass big enough for the simplest games of even the smallest children. It is a common sight during any afternoon or evening to see dozens of little children in this section of the neighborhood huddled together in some grimy alley or chasing one another around a telephone pole on the street corner—human nature, both metaphorically and literally, being torn around by the hair of the head.

XI. EDUCATION AND JUVENILE DELINQUENCY

For a general conception of the educational status of this neighborhood the reader is referred to Table XXIV.[1]

TABLE XXIV

PERCENTAGE OF NON-SCHOOL ATTENDANCE BY WARDS OF CHILDREN 6 TO 20 YEARS OF AGE

Ward	No. Attending	No. Not Attending	Percentage Not Attending
8	676	4	0.6
16	2,945	251	7.8
5	2,945	402	12.0
7	1,718	325	15.8
6	1,394	478	16.6
15	1,668	357	17.6
14	1,588	374	19.1
4	2,096	519	19.8
12	812	202	19.9
11	3,032	761	20.1
1	2,634	704	21.1
10	2,088	704	25.2
3	2,974	1,125	27.4
13	2,705	1,299	32.4
2	1,528	963	38.7
9	742	586	44.1

Recalling that our neighborhood is located in Wards 9 and 10, it is evident that a relatively large percentage of its young people are not attending school. Ward 9 stands at the bottom of the list with 44.1 per cent of the age group in question not attending school. Ward 10 occupies the fifth place from the bottom, with a percentage of non-school attendance of 25.2.

There is no way of finding out what proportion of the non-school attendance of each ward falls in the lower years of the age group. Obviously, however, the largest part of it is made up of children over fourteen years of age. The different percentages just indi-

[1] These figures are taken from the unpublished records of the Columbus Board of Education, 1918.

cated may be taken, therefore, as a rough measure of the extent to which the young people of the various wards of the city go to high school or college. Ward 8 might be omitted from the list inasmuch as it comprises the central business section of the city and has but few children resident in it. Moreover, Wards 2, 3, and 13 with their relatively poor showing should be studied in connection with Map I[1] which shows the distribution of national and racial groups within the city. It will be observed that these are areas in which reside large negro and foreign elements.

No attempt was made to obtain information relative to the question of retardation of the children of the schools in the neighborhood. But in a recent study, made by the department of psychology of the state university, the children of Fieser School were rated as mentally two years below the average for children of the same age in a school located in one of the higher economic areas of the city.[2]

Fieser School.—The two elementary schools, Fieser and Franklinton, are both very much overcrowded. The Fieser School tries to obviate this condition by dividing its elementary classes into two sections, one attending from 8 to 11.30 A.M., and the other from 12:30 to 3 P.M. The school has an open-window or "fresh-air" class which on the date of inspection had an enrolment of eighteen pupils. These pupils attend school from 8 A.M. to 3 P.M. and are served their noonday meal by the school under the direction of Dr. Lenhart, the physician in charge. Penny lunches are served at the Fieser School at 10 A.M. daily. The principal states that about 25 per cent of the children patronize these lunches, which consist of a glass of whole milk and some graham crackers. The school also conducts a special class for retarded children. This class has an enrolment of sixteen children, most of whom are colored.[3]

Juvenile delinquency.—The reader is referred to Map V[1] for a general idea of the territorial distribution of the "official" cases of juvenile delinquency for a single year period, 1918–19. The follow-

[1] See *American Journal of Sociology,* XXVII (September, 1921), 147.

[2] J. W. Bridges and Lillian Coler, "The Relation of Intelligence to Social Status," *Psychology Review,* XXIV (January, 1917), p. 22.

[3] See *American Journal Sociology,* XXVII (September, 1921), 166.

ing map of the neighborhood shows the local distribution of delinquency in greater detail. Of the 521 cases of juvenile delinquency indicated on the map of the city, 36 fall within the confines of the neighborhood. While this is a larger pro rata percentage than for

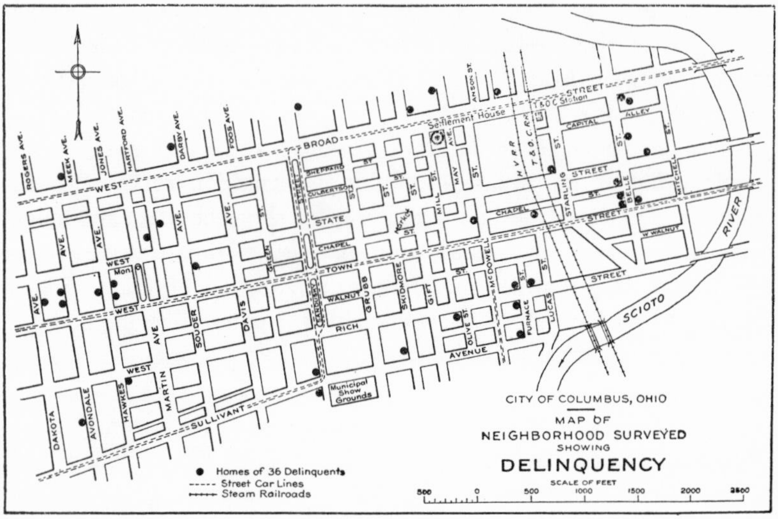

Map XIII

the city as a whole, still the neighborhood shows up favorably when compared with some of the other local divisions of the city.

XII. NEIGHBORHOOD SENTIMENT

In the course of time every section and quarter of a city takes on something of the character and quality of its inhabitants. Each separate part of the city is inevitably stained with the peculiar sentiments of its population. The effect of this is to convert what was at first a mere geographical expression into a neighborhood, that is to say, a locality with sentiments, traditions, and a history of its own.[1]

Attachment to locality is probably the best criterion of positive neighborhood sentiment. There is a tendency on the part of most people after living for a time in a certain spot or locality to become so psychologically adjusted to their physical and social surroundings that they experience a feeling of discomfort and dissatisfaction when transferred to a new environment. We are all familiar with

[1] Park, *op. cit.*, p. 579.

the homesickness of the young person on the event of his first departure from his native village and his longing to return at the first opportunity to what he considers to be "the best spot on earth." In the city environment neighborhood sentiment, or attachment to locality, has become largely dissipated owing to the transitory nature of residence and the absence of home ownership. But various sections of city life differ remarkably in regard to the extent of local feeling and neighborhood pride exhibited. In some localities within the city, neighborhood sentiment is a negative factor, expressing itself in terms of disapproval and repulsion with regard to local surroundings, while in other areas the opposite sentiments prevail, those of local pride and loyalty.

From the standpoint of neighborhood organization it is important to know the general attitudes of the people toward their physical and social surroundings. Where there exists general satisfaction with respect to locality it is possible to enlist interest in neighborhood up-building. But if the opposite sentiments prevail, those of dissatisfaction and disapproval, it is not likely that much headway can be made in building up interest in neighborhood institutions.

An attempt was made in our survey to obtain from every household the prevailing attitude toward the neighborhood and the people living round about. Direct questions were avoided, but in the course of conversation the visitor recorded significant statements made by the informant pertaining to the physical and social surroundings. Obviously it is impracticable to attempt to classify the great variety of remarks quoted by the investigators. We have selected almost at random, therefore, two streets, one from the eastern half of the neighborhood and one from the western half. The schedules are taken in order for these two streets and the sentiments expressed in the words of the informant are recorded without selection or discrimination. Street A lies west of Sandusky Street where over 50 per cent of the residents own their homes. Street B, on the other hand, is located in the more broken-down region near the eastern end of the neighborhood where less than 25 per cent of the residents own their homes.

The following lists give the direct expressions of neighborhood sentiment for the two streets in question:

STREET A

We like the neighborhood very much.

Perfectly satisfied, afraid I'll have to get out now because of property exchanges and I'm very sorry I have to leave.

Like it pretty well—very nice neighbors.

Very good dear neighbors, no time for visiting.

Like it very much, not uppish but very friendly.

Fine neighborhood, couldn't be better for us.

Very pleasant neighborhood.

Neighborhood seems attractive.

Satisfied with neighborhood, and like my neighbors very much.

Satisfied with neighborhood.

I like neighborhood very much, prefer it to any other I know of.

Pleasant people but not well acquainted with them.

I like it, all good friends in neighborhood.

Grand neighborhood, people very friendly but I do not visit much.

Don't have time for visiting.

Like my neighbors very much.

Very nice neighbors and neighborhood.

Don't visit back and forth very much but all good friends.

Got right kind of neighbors, just like one family in helping each other.

Neighborhood couldn't be better.

There never was a better set of neighbors, all willing to help each other.

Very much attached to this neighborhood.

There is a great deal of good spirit and friendliness in our neighborhood.

Splendid neighborhood, I like my neighbors, but do not visit with them a great deal.

Perfectly satisfied with the neighborhood; neighbors are all nice friendly people.

STREET B

Neighborhood just average, people strange and quarrel a lot.

I don't like it and don't mix with the neighbors but have to stay on account of my boy.

Rough district, I don't speak to the neighbors, they swear and drink too much. They are jealous of us.

Would like to move out east again.

Like West Side but not this street, no freedom, I hate Mrs. K.

Don't like neighbors, they are hard to get along with, fussy, so I stay to myself and bother none of them.

Don't like neighborhood, want to move away, too many low characters.
My husband likes East Side better but will stay here though with me.
Don't go out much here, don't like my neighbors.
I like the neighborhood and have good neighbors.
Neighborhood fine, don't have much time to visit neighbors.
I like the few neighbors I know.
Like the neighborhood.
No hard feelings among neighbors.
Don't like it but have to put up with it.
Like West Side but not this street, every one gets along fine but Mrs. ——.
Like it very well, have good neighbors.
Don't like it here, don't speak to the neighbors.
Not well acquainted, don't go any place.
Like the neighborhood very well.
I like the one neighbor that I know all right.
I like Rich Street better, people here think they're better than I am.
I know all the neighbors but don't bother with them at all.
Haven't been here long but like the neighbors so far.
We speak to each other but don't visit at all.

It is obvious that the term "neighborhood" in these expressions is used in the restricted sense as implying, for the most part, the street on which the family resides, or at most not more than the immediately adjacent streets. And the "neighbors" are the people living on the same street with perhaps the families on the street in the rear whose back doors are adjacent.

There is a striking difference in the warmth of the sentiments exhibited in these two lists. Street A is a street of neighbors; a street of wholesome common folk who have lived long in close proximity and have developed sentiments of loyalty and attachment to their local environment. Street B, on the other hand, with the exception of a few families in the middle which form, as one might say, a "warm spot" of neighborly association, represents the result of a forced selection. That is where economic necessity compels people of unlike attitudes and cultural tastes to live in close proximity to one another. In such regions there can be no positive neighborhood sentiment; hatred and avoidance prevail until opportunity arises for moving on.

THE NEIGHBORHOOD: A STUDY OF LOCAL LIFE IN THE CITY OF COLUMBUS, OHIO—*Concluded*

R. D. McKENZIE
University of Washington

ABSTRACT

Our system of government is based upon the assumption of the territorial group as a unit. Modern means of communication and transportation have to a considerable extent nullified the significance of spatial proximity as a group bond. All the traditional forms of political and social organization are affected thereby. Wards and administrative districts of cities as a rule have no correlation with natural groupings of population. Thus the influence of local opinion in social control is minimized. City populations tend to segregate into territorial publics having similar attitudes on questions pertaining to the mores. Such similarity of attitude is not so pronounced on economic questions. Rehabilitation of neighborhood sentiment in a city is a difficult problem. Anything that tends to stabilize residence and give to the neighborhood a unitary character may serve to develop neighborhood consciousness.

PART III. SOCIAL RECONSTRUCTION OF THE NEIGHBORHOOD

XIII. THE NEIGHBORHOOD AS THE UNIT OF POLITICAL AND SOCIAL REFORM

Our entire system of government, municipal, state, and national, is based on the assumption of the locality group as the unit of representation and administration. This, of course, is an inheritance from earlier times when geographical proximity was the one fundamental basis of group life. But modern means of communication and transportation together with the recent development of large interest groups whose common interest transcends geographical boundaries have undermined the foundations of our political system and have complicated all our problems of social reform. This is especially true with reference to affairs of administration in our large cities, where the dominant interest groups prevail and where life for the majority is precarious and transitory.

Localities do not stand for special interests, being areas of community which circumscribe only a very limited and, with the extension of community less and less definite exclusiveness of social type and interest. It is in very great measure the mere convenience of contiguity rather than the intrinsic distinctiveness of local interests which makes the locality an effective social unit. But in the central association that convenience no longer counts, and here organization by local divisions is, except under special circumstances, a mere impediment to the activity of the association. The case of representative government has interest in this connection. While the unit of election remains locality, the division of interest within the central legislature scarcely ever follows the lines of locality. Consequently it becomes very difficult to attain any form of true representation on the basis of local election. Members ostensibly elected to represent a locality, often in fact represent, though inadequately on account of the mode of election, not merely the broad policy of a party, but the special interest of some association, some trade or profession or church or other grouping. This cross representation is creating one of the most difficult problems within the sphere of political science.[1]

In general the criticisms of our city government, as far as they pertain to the neighborhood, may be divided into two classes. First, the excessive localism revealed by some of the more stable and stronger city neighborhoods tends to exploit the larger interests of the city in general. This type of situation is illustrated in the following quotation from the *Pittsburgh Survey*.

It is not suprising, therefore, that Pittsburgh early became a hotbed of petty politics. As in other cities councilmen chosen by wards throve through catering to local needs while indifferent or negligent to the weightier interests of the city as a whole. Thus, whole sections of well-paved streets might mark the bailiwick of some aggressive ward councilman, who none the less had a hand in giving these same streets along with the main thorofares of Pittsburgh, in perpetuity to the street car monopoly. Hence the saying: "Any ward can be bought for a new side walk or a pair of wooden stairs." Local benefit naturally became the test of discharge of official duty, the street paving schedule, the pork barrel of the city budget. . . . . Even justice has been so diverse an interest that each ward chooses its own local magistrate, before whom, none the less, may be brought a case from anywhere in the city. The only concern of an alderman is to please his "constits"; let him "soak" the fellow outside his district and his re-election was secure.[2]

On the other hand, the utter lack of neighborhood sentiment, so common in many sections of our large cities, provides a fruitful field for the establishment of our notorious boss system of government. The boss seizes upon the opportunity to act the part of the good neighbor among an element of the population whose precari-

[1] R. M. Maciver, *Community* (1917), p. 258.

[2] *Pittsburgh Survey*, I, 45–46.

ous conditions of life emphasize the value of the kindly, personal, neighborly relations, but at the same time create indifference toward the more general interests of the neighborhood or community as a whole.

A successful ward boss must be a worker, capable by his example of inspiring others to similar industry. He must not be content with doing the work that comes to him, he must look for things to do. As his work consists mainly in doing favors for voters, he must inspire requests as well as grant them. Therefore he encourages voters to come to him for help when they are out of work or in any other sort of trouble. When a voter is arrested, the ward or district leader will lend his services to secure bail or to provide counsel, or will arrange to have the offender's fine paid for him. Then there are the day-to-day favors which the local boss stands ready to do for all who come to him, provided they are voters or can influence voters. These services cannot be even recapitulated here, for their name is legion. To one he lends money to stall a landlord whose patience is exhausted; to a family of another he sends fuel or provisions in time of need. "He buys medicine for the sick and helps to bury the dead. He dispenses an ample hospitality in the saloons; as soon as he comes in, known and unknown, gather about him, and he treats everybody. He is the only one who does not drink, for he is on duty." Tested by his acts, the boss is chief among neighborhood philanthropists; judged by the motives that prompt his acts, he is a serpent spreading the slime of political debauchery over whole sections of the community. With the submerged tenth (it would be more accurately termed the submerged half) of a great city's population, however, it is the acts and not the motives of the man that weigh.[1]

Students of municipal affairs disagree concerning plans for the reconstruction of city government. Some authorities, recognizing the present disorganized state of the city neighborhood, advocate the selection of representatives at large without respect to neighborhood or vocational interests;[2] others would even go so far as to abolish entirely the geographical unit of representation and substitute for it representation on the basis of vocational or interest groups;[3] while others again, realizing the importance of neighborhood sentiment as a civic force, would attempt to rehabilitate and revivify the neighborhood making it function once more as a

[1] Munro, *The Government of American Cities*, pp. 175–76.

[2] This is the position taken by exponents of commission government. Cf. E. S. Bradford, *Commission Government in American Cities* (1911), p. 305.

[3] For a concise statement of the views of the "Political Pluralists" see M. P. Follett, *The New State* (1920), chap. xxviii.

community institution.[1] There is general agreement, however, that our present ward system of representation is a failure.

The ward councillor represents his own ward, and that alone. He forgets that the city is more than the sum of its wards, and that the public opinion of the city may be different from the totality of neighborhood clamors. Ward divisions are at best ephemeral: unlike the French *arrondissement*, the American ward has rarely any traditions and as a unit of area exacts no spontaneous loyalty from the people who live in it. What passes for ward loyalty is, more commonly than not, local prejudice fostered by politicians to serve their own personal ends. Moreover, the concentration of single ethnic elements in particular sections of the city makes it practically certain that, under the ward system, some members of the council will owe their election to nothing but their proficiency in appealing to racial or religious or social narrowness. The ward system likewise affords a standing incentive to that most vicious of all American contributions to the science of practical politics, the gerrymander; it makes possible the control of a majority in the council by a minority of the city's voters, and, unless redistricting is resorted to frequently, it fosters gross inequalities in representation. The term "ward" has accordingly come into disrepute in the terminology of American government, a somewhat curious fact, by the way, since in England, where councillors are and always have been chosen from wards, no such odium has been developed. Its presence here is doubtless explained by the fact that in American ward representation, ward politics, and ward organization have come to be associated in the public mind with bossism, trickery, and almost everything else that is politically demoralizing. A feeling so deeply lodged can scarcely be without some substantial foundation.[2]

Although the territorial unit of representation is tending to become a thing of the past in American city government, yet the unit for administrative purposes still remains the geographical area. Cities are districted into a large number of local units to meet the

[1] M. P. Follett is one of the best-known advocates of the rehabilitation of the neighborhood as a political and social unit. The thesis of her recent book, *The New State*, is that intelligent participation in social control can be achieved only through the conscious reconstruction and federation of such small territorial groups as the neighborhood.

As a unit of social reform, the neighborhood has received the attention of social workers for several decades. The social settlement movement represents the first attempt to institutionalize the social activities of the neighborhood. The present trend of this movement is evidenced in the increasing popularity of the social center activities, community councils, and, in a still more comprehensive way, in the social Unit Plan of Cincinnati.

[2] Munro, *The Government of American Cities*, pp. 191–92.

administrative problems of the various departments of city government. Each department subdivides the city into geographical units adjusted to suit its peculiar administrative purposes without respect to the natural groupings of population, and without consideration of the geographical subdivisions made by other departments of city government.

Attention has been called to the fact that one of the things which make city government inherently difficult, is the lack of neighborhood feeling which seems invariably to be produced by city life. If each branch of the city government, and each city executive department, forms districts to suit its own convenience merely, it is almost a certainty that there will be almost as many series of different districts as there are branches of city government and city executive departments. The result is that such a neighborhood feeling as may exist is disintegrated, and that it becomes impossible, so long as this administrative diversity continues, for such a neighborhood feeling to develop. If, on the other hand, care were taken to make the election districts the same as the judicial districts and to cause these to conform, in some way, to the police, fire, and other districts, if the district court-house, the fire engine-house, the police station-house, and even the school-house in given parts of the city were situated, from the point of view of city geography, near each other—placed perhaps in or around a small playground or park,—it would be possible to develop civic centers which would tend to encourage the development of neighborhood spirit. It is quite true that the convenience of the departments might be interfered with, but the loss suffered by the departments would be more than compensated for by the development of neighborhood spirit, and in many instances as well by the greater convenience of the citizen who would find that his business with the city government could be conducted with greater ease than under conditions where the city districts bore no relation to each other. Under the plan which has been outlined, of course the districts would be more permanent than at present, while the civic centers which might develop would, of necessity, be absolutely permanent. The changes of population which are going on so continuously in the city would make the problem of district representation a different one from what it is where the districts are not permanent but are changed to suit the changes of population. The problem would not, however, be one of great difficulty, for, instead of establishing single districts as at present, it would be possible to make provision for districts whose representation would vary with their population.

The plan which has been outlined is one which to a large degree has been adopted in Paris. Paris is divided into twenty districts, each of which has a civic center—*the mairie*—at which are found the office of the *maire*, in this case a district and not a city officer—generally a city library, and the local office of the charities department. The *mairie* itself is usually situated in a small open space or park. The twenty districts, in addition to being thus administrative districts, are also election and judicial districts. In this case, notwithstanding their differences in population, they are equally represented on the city council. So far, however, in the United States little attention seems to have been given by the city governments to this important matter, and the convenience of the administrative departments alone has been considered. The result is that an opportunity has not been availed of either to preserve or to develop neighborhood feeling, or to secure an architectural effect which would render city life much more attractive than it is at present.[1]

If the neighborhood is ever to be organized as a political or social unit, it is of the utmost importance that the formal superstructure shall be made to coincide as nearly as possible with the natural neighborhood groupings of the population. It is a remarkable fact that the most prominent advocates of neighborhood reconstruction have failed to take cognizance of this necessity. It is surely apparent that any effective system of community planning must take account of the divergent attitudes of the various community groups; and this is just as important with respect to the locality groups as it is with respect to the trade union or chamber of commerce.

It is, of course, not always an easy problem to locate the boundaries of natural neighborhood groups. Frequently one neighborhood blends into another without any objective signs of demarcation. On the other hand, areas of similar objective characteristics may be inhabitated by family groups whose interests and attitudes are entirely irreconcilable.

I shall now present the results of an attempt to study neighborhood group attitudes in the city of Columbus. My study is based on data obtained from the records of the Board of Elections. The geographical units for the collecting and recording of data on all subjects on which the city's electorate votes are the precincts and wards. Columbus is divided into sixteen wards having a total of 262 precincts. The precinct is quite small, including but one or two city blocks and having an average registered electorate of less than two hundred.

[1] Frank J. Goodnow, *City Government in the United States* (1906), pp. 201–3.

I shall attempt to discover the territorial distribution of the voting public[1] son a number of issues which have come before the electorate during the past few years. Municipal questions divide the voting public into two groups—those in favor and those opposed. After a campaign which varies in intensity according to the nature of the issue, a vote is taken and the result apparently accepted by both sides. The geographical distribution of the losing minority seems of little consequence. From the standpoint of law enforcement, however, it becomes a very significant matter whether one city neighborhood has imposed its will on a numerically smaller neighborhood entirely out of sympathy with the decision. Without the support of the local opinion of the neighborhood it becomes extremely difficult to enforce legislative enactments. If, on the other hand, the losing minority does not happen to be segregated in particular neighborhoods, but is scattered evenly throughout the city, the question of law enforcement is of a much more simple nature.

In order to ascertain the types of municipal questions on which local segregation of voters takes place, I have made a study of the voting records on eight different issues on which the electorate of Columbus have voted during the past few years. The percentage of affirmative votes on each of the eight municipal questions recorded in Table XXV has been determined for each ward. The results are compared with the percentage of the affirmative votes on each issue for the city as a whole. The deviations of each ward from the city's average is thus taken as a measure of the ward segregation of voters on each question.

This table shows very distinctly that there is much greater segregation of voters on subjects pertaining to the mores, or social customs, than on subjects which deal with economic questions. In the first group of subjects, designated Class A, the ward deviations from the city's average range from 6 to 12—a fact which shows that there is a very pronounced local bunching of similar attitudes on

[1] Any unorganized association of individuals bound together by common opinions, sentiments, or desires and too numerous for each to maintain personal relations with the others, constitutes a public in the broadest sense of the term."—W. J. Shepard, "Public Opinion," *Amer. Jour. of Sociol.*, XV, 36.

TABLE XXV

AVERAGE DEVIATIONS OF WARD VOTES FROM THE GENERAL AVERAGE FOR COLUMBUS

Subject	Wards																Average Dev. for All Wards
	1	2	3	4	5	6	7	8	9	10	11	12	13	14	15	16	
Class A:																	
Prohibition (1917).....	− 8.8	−30.9	−17.8	−4.8	+10.8	+5.1	+ .8	−12.1	−22.8	−7.7	+12.7	−13.3	+ .3	+1.1	+24.9	+24.3	12.4
Prohibition (1918).....	−11.4	−30.5	−16.0	−3.7	+10.7	+6.2	−2.0	− 7.7	−23.0	−7.7	+12.3	−17.8	− .9	+ .7	+23.6	+22.3	12.3
Poolroom ordinance (1917)............	− 6.5	−15.3	− 9.7	+ .8	+ 7.2	+ .6	−2.0	− 5.1	−10.6	−5.0	+ 3.3	− 8.0	−3.8	+ .4	+13.2	+11.3	6.4
Woman's suffrage (1917)............	− 6.9	−26.1	−12.3	−2.7	+ 7.5	+4.0	−1.8	−10.8	−19.2	−4.7	+ 7.1	−14.1	− .6	.....	+19.9	+20.9	9.9
To prohibit employment of women in places where liquor is sold (1918)............	− 4.4	−20.9	−10.1	+4.0	+10.1	+7.3	+1.5	− 4.1	−20.3	−2.7	+11.6	−11.2	+2.7	+2.4	+22.7	+18.9	9.7
Class B:																	
City tax levy (1917)...	− 7.3	− 7.9	−10.5	+2.5	+ 4.6	+ .8	+2.0	+2.7	+ 1.7	+ .3	− 4.0	+ .5	−2.8	+3.0	+11.9	+ 4.4	4.2
City tax levy (1918)....	− 1.3	− 4.5	− 5.9	+3.3	+ 3.8	+ .6	−1.5	+ 5.7	+ 4.7	+ .3	− 2.7	+ 2.9	−3.7	+2.1	+ 5.0	+ 1.6	3.5
School bond issue (1917)	− 4.7	− 5.2	− 7.8	−1.1	− 1.1	+4.7	+3.2	+ 2.8	+ 9.6	−1.6	− 2.7	+ 4.6	+ .8	+4.1	+ 5.7	+ 1.4	3.4
City school tax levy (1918)............	− 7.3	− 7.3	− 8.0	+2.1	+ 5.4	+1.6	−3.1	+ 2.7	− .2	−1.4	− 3.2	− 1.1	−2.6	+2.3	+ 9.4	+ 6.8	4.0

these questions. Wards 15 and 16, which show the highest positive deviations, stand in striking contrast to Wards 2, 3, and 9, which show almost as large negative deviations from the average for the city as a whole. With respect to the economic issues, grouped in Class B, the ward deviations from the city's average are relatively slight. On no subject is the average deviation for all the wards in Class B as great as that found for any of the issues in Class A. The most conspicuous bunching of opposites is found in Wards 3 and 15, especially on the city tax levy issue of 1917.

Although small deviations are found on the School Bond issue of 1917, nevertheless, from the standpoint of community interest and campaign enthusiasm, this was an unusually hotly contested local issue. The two publics concerned, however, were geographically dispersed almost uniformly over the entire city. Athough the final vote stood 9,738 for, to 22,918 against, not a single precinct in the city voted a majority in favor of the proposed bond issue.

There seems to be little correlation between high economic status and the tendency to support measures involving an increase in taxation. While Wards 4 and 5 rank highest in the city with respect to economic status, still, on the average, they do not support economic measures as well as Ward 9 which stands at the bottom of the economic scale for the city. Furthermore, it is interesting to note that the deviations of Wards 1, 2, and 3, wards which comprise the large German neighborhood, are negative on all questions listed in our table; while the deviations in Wards 14, 15, and 16 are positive on all issues. Wards 9 and 10[1] have negative deviations on all issues in Class A but tend to support taxation measures. This may be partially accounted for by the relatively small number of large taxpayers in these wards.

Let us now examine more closely the territorial distribution of the publics supporting and opposing each of the foregoing subjects grouped in Class A, as representing the mores, that is, questions involving conceptions of right and wrong. Of course the ward is too large a geographical unit to furnish a true picture of the details of local sentiment on these subjects. Local groups of diametrically opposite points of view are frequently bunched together within the

[1] These wards embrace the disorganized neighborhood already studied.

same ward. The precinct, therefore, is a better unit than the ward, to bring into relief the natural boundaries of the local group. In order to illustrate the various regional attitudes on questions pertaining to the mores I have prepared Maps XIV, XV, and XVI.

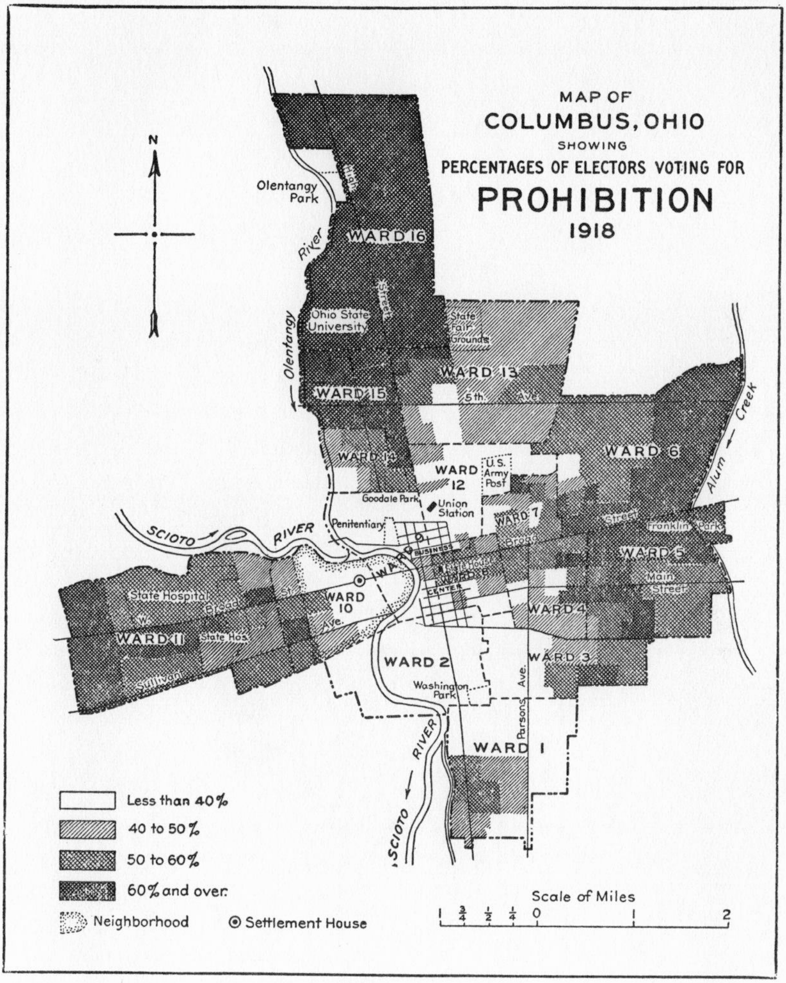

Map XIV

These maps are constructed on the basis of the voting precinct and represent the percentage of electors for each precinct voting affirmatively on the three subjects in question—prohibition, woman's suffrage, and the non-employment of women in liquor shops.

The similarity of shading of the various sections of the city in all three of these maps is significant. The local areas that supported

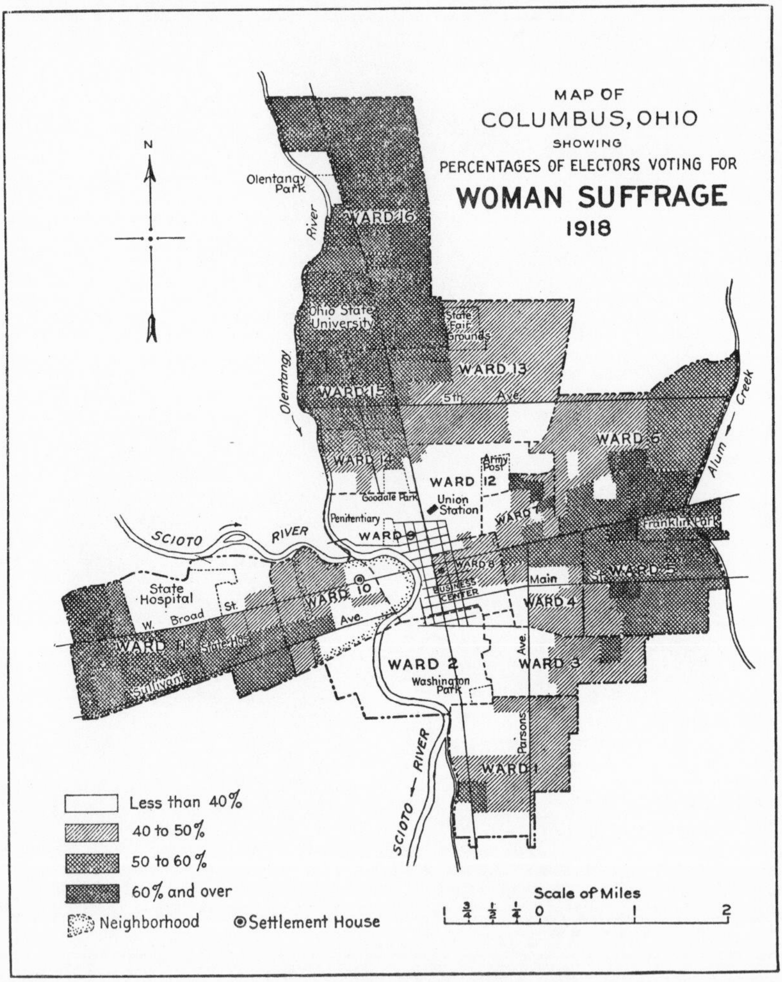

MAP XV

prohibition invariably supported woman's suffrage to approximately the same degree. The areas surrounding the central business section of the city stand out conspicuously as opposed to both prohibition and woman's suffrage and in favor of the employment of women in liquor shops; while the eastern, western, and northern extremities of the city—the three leading residential areas—are

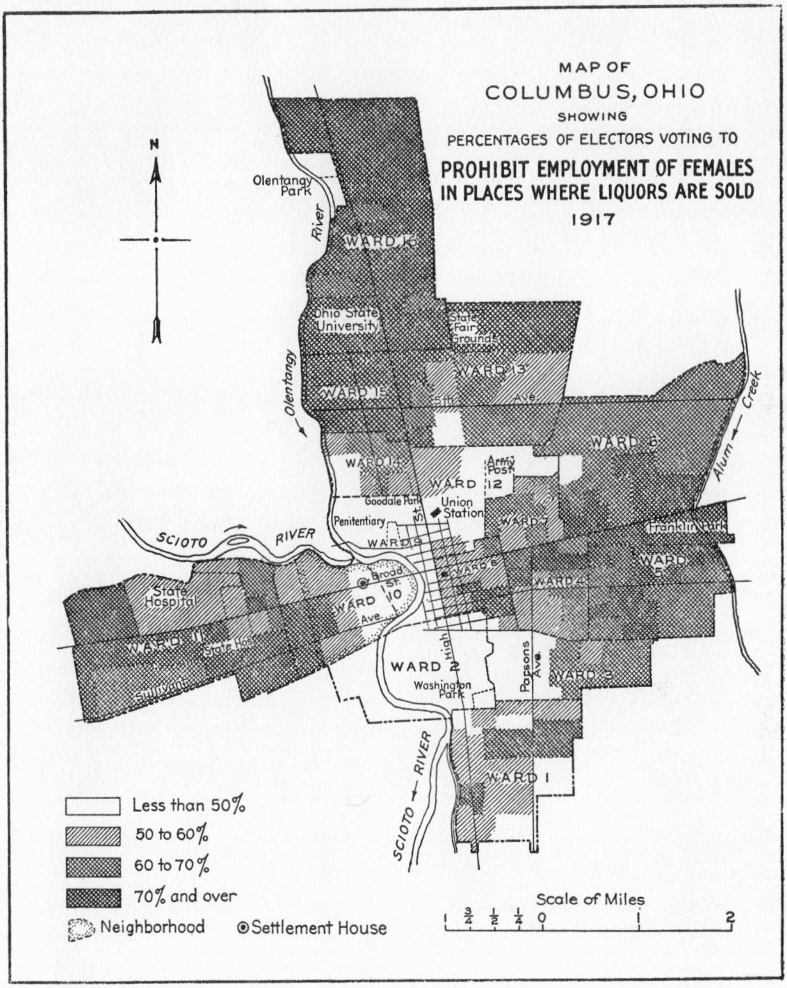

MAP XVI

strong supporters of the first two issues and opposers of the third issue.

In the process of the sifting and sorting of population within a city, there is a tendency for people of similar mores to become grouped together in neighborhood association.[1] And it is only in the decision of questions involving the mores that the specific group character of these local areas comes into prominence. The consistency of attitudes displayed by the various local regions on questions dealing with the mores is remarkable. Not only did the Columbus vote on prohibition for consecutive years show almost precisely the same results, as far as local segregation of opinion is concerned, but the votes on the other subjects, more or less kindred, show almost identical distribution of supporters and opposers. The ward distribution of opinion on a number of such subjects is graphically shown in Graph I.

The points are arbitrarily connected to assist the eye in following the ward fluctuations on these subjects. The correlation of ward opinions on these three subjects is conspicious. Obviously the voter who favored woman's suffrage voted also for prohibition, and for the non-employment of women in liquor shops.

The lower line graphically representing the relative economic status of the different wards, bears an interesting similarity of fluctuations to those of the lines illustrating ward opinion on the three subjects in question. Wards 4, 5, 15, and 16, which stand high in economic status are the strongest supporters of each of the three municipal issues; while Ward 9, which has the lowest economic rating, shows the lowest affirmative vote on these issues.

The correlation of opinion on these subjects may be shown still more clearly by observing the precinct distribution of votes for a single ward. There are too many precincts to make it practicable to show this distribution for the entire city. But the distribution of opinion within one ward will serve as an example of the general

[1] Similarity of attitudes, however, is not in itself a criterion of group consciousness. It is necessary that the individual members of the group shall be aware of the similarity of their attitudes. Referring to the Polish peasant, Thomas and Znaniecki, say, "The manner in which social opinion holds the community together is easily analyzed. Any extraordinary occurrence becomes for a certain time the focus of attention of all the members of the community, an identical attitude toward this is developed, and each member of the community is conscious that he shares the general attitude or that his attitude is shared by the rest of the community. These are the three original elements of the mechanism of social opinion: the phenomenon, the identity of attitude, and the consciousness of this identity."—*The Polish Peasant in Europe and America*, I, 145.

GRAPH I

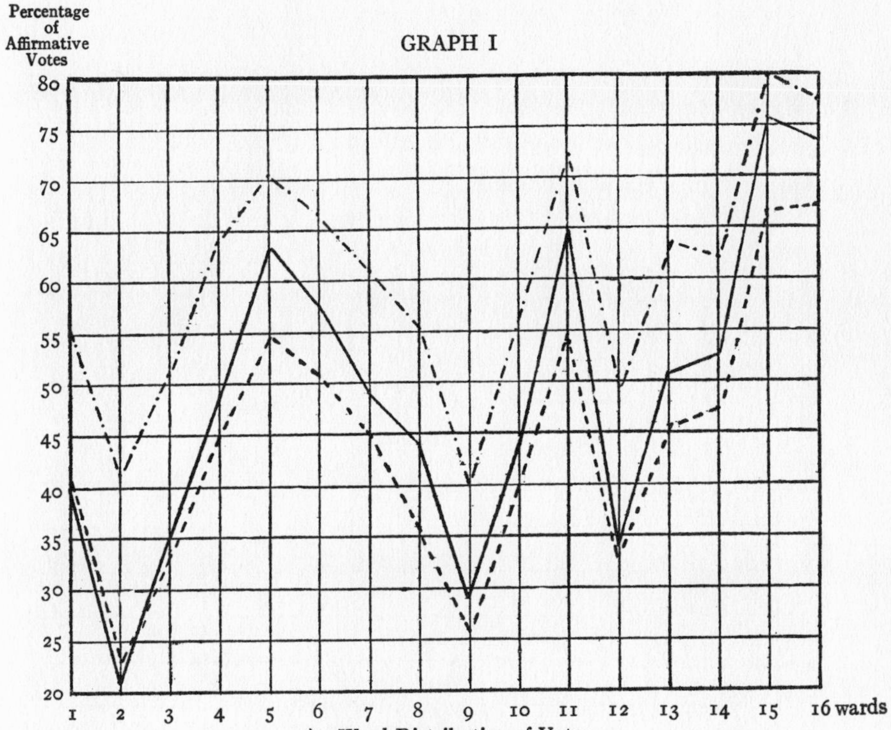

a) Ward Distribution of Votes

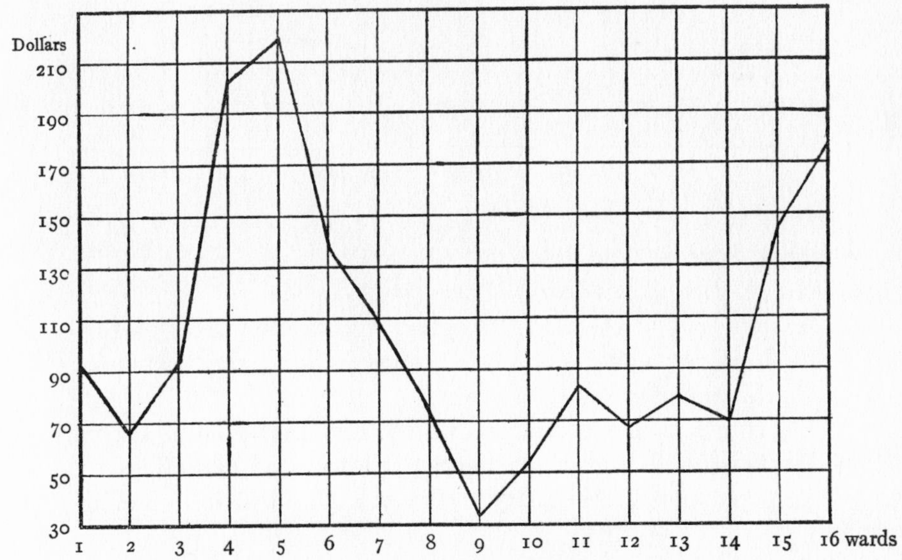

b) Economic Status of Wards

NOTE.—Economic status is determined by dividing total tax returns, per ward, on household furniture by total number of electors per ward.

tendency. Graph II indicates the percentage of voters in each precinct in Ward 3, who voted in favor of the three issues: woman's suffrage, prohibition, and the non-employment of women in places where liquor is sold.

While the percentages of affirmative votes do not fluctuate similarly in every case still it is very plain that there is a direct

GRAPH II

Precinct Distribution of Votes on Three Issues—Ward 3

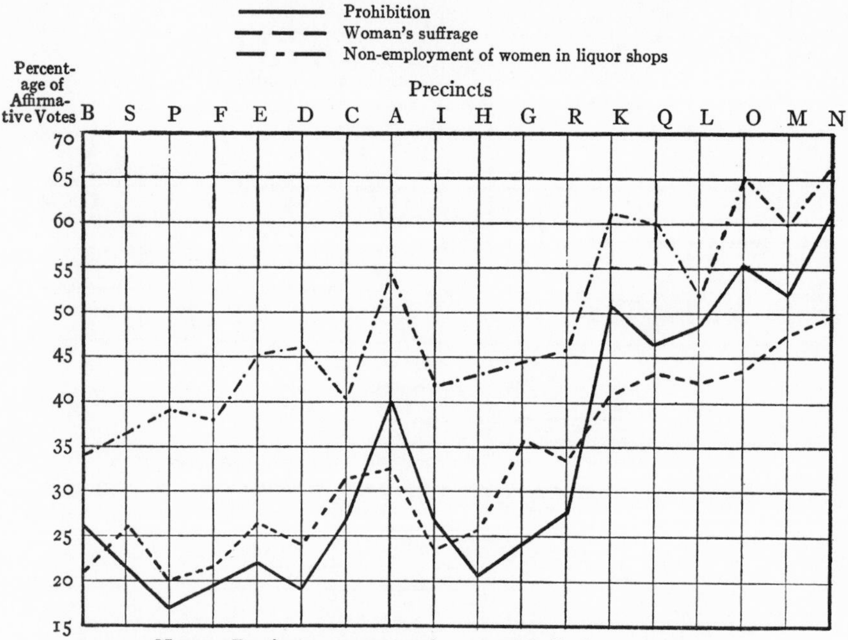

NOTE.—Precincts are arranged geographically from west to east

correlation of opinion on these three issues. Moreover, it is evident that there is a decided regional divergence of opinion within the boundaries of this ward. Precincts M, N, and O, which lie in the eastern end of the ward, represent opposite attitudes to those of such precincts as B and S, which occupy the western section of the ward, bordering on Sixth Street.

It is clear to everyone that ward boundaries, as a rule, are purely artificial, and do not, therefore, represent the natural groupings of population within a city. However, all wards in Columbus are

TABLE XXVI

AVERAGE DEVIATIONS OF PRECINCT VOTES FROM THE AVERAGES OF THE DIFFERENT WARDS

Subjects	Wards																Average Deviation for All Wards
	1	2	3	4	5	6	7	8	9	10	11	12	13	14	15	16	
1. Prohibition (1918)	7.8	2.9	12.7	7.7	5.4	6.9	6.7	6.9	6.5	8.4	7.0	7.0	8.9	6.7	5.8	5.8	7.1
2. Woman's suffrage (1918)	6.3	3.8	9.2	6.3	4.0	7.9	8.0	9.2	4.7	6.3	6.5	5.8	6.9	6.8	6.3	6.3	6.5
3. To prohibit employment of women in places where liquor is sold	4.9	4.4	8.7	5.4	4.3	7.3	4.3	7.5	5.6	7.1	6.2	6.4	6.4	6.2	4.7	4.7	6.0
4. Governor (1918)	4.7	4.0	6.3	6.4	5.7	14.9	15.6	9.7	12.2	4.8	7.4	12.1	8.6	5.4	4.2	4.2	8.1
Average for each ward	5.9	3.8	9.2	6.4	4.9	9.2	8.6	8.3	7.2	6.6	6.8	7.8	7.7	6.6	6.3	5.2	....

not equally artificial. Some show a much greater tendency toward homogeneity and coincidence with natural local groupings than others. In order to discover the comparative homogeneity of the different wards of Columbus I have made a study of the precinct variations of opinion for each ward. The method employed was as follows; the total percentage of affirmative votes in each ward on each of the four subjects indicated on Table XXVI, was taken as the basis. Then the percentage of affirmative votes on each subject for each precinct within the ward was compared with this, and the deviations averaged. Table XXVI gives the result of this tabulation for all the wards of the city.

A few interesting facts are revealed in this table. In the first place it is quite clear that there is considerable difference in the extent of solidarity in the various wards of the city. Ward 2 stands out conspicuously as distinctly the most homogeneous ward. With its average deviation on all subjects of but 3.8, it stands in striking contrast to its neighboring Ward 3, which has an average deviation of 9.2; and to Ward 6, which has an equally high average. In fact Ward 2 consistently shows greater homogeneity on all issues than any other ward in the city, with the two slight exceptions of Wards 5 and 7, in item three, and in these particular cases the differences are extremely small.

The precinct deviations from the ward averages for Wards 2 and 3 are graphically represented in Graph III.

With the single exception of Precinct A, which stands at the northeast corner of the ward, there is extremely little geographical bunching of votes in Ward 2. Ward 3, on the other hand, shows the opposite tendency. Its precinct fluctuations vary from 17 to 62 per cent of the electors voting in favor of prohibition.

The superior homogeneity of Ward 2 is due to the fact that this ward is inhabitated almost exclusively by a single nationality, Germans. Ward 3, on the contrary, is composed of a number of different foreign groups in addition to a large American population.

XIV. CONCLUSIONS

A few conclusions may be drawn from this study of local opinion. First, the population of a city tends to segregate itself into locality groups possessing similar cultural and moral values; second, issues involving economic expenditure reveal more reflection and personal choice on the part of the voter than do issues pertaining to the mores; third, the ward is not a unit of opinion on any issue except where its boundaries happen to coincide with the natural cultural and ethnic groupings of the population.

Those interested in the rehabilitation of the city neighborhood must, if they are to succeed, take into consideration the dominant

GRAPH III

Comparative Homogeneity of Wards 2 and 3

As illustrated by precinct distribution of affirmative votes on the issue of prohibition, 1918

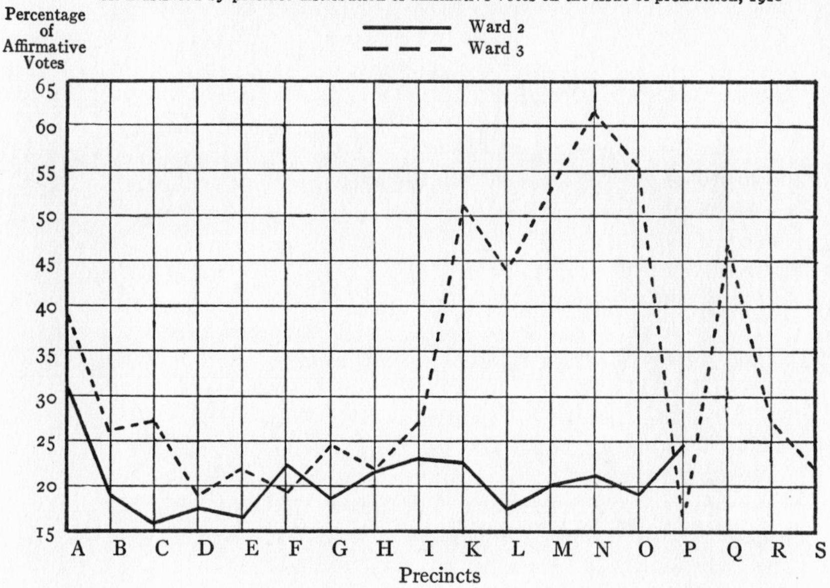

forces at work strengthening or disintegrating the locality groups. An efficient scheme of neighborhood reconstruction must take cognizance of the natural groupings of the population, and efforts must be made to stabilize such groupings as far as possible by establishing community safeguards against encroaching disturbing factors. On the other hand, efforts must be made to give to each neighborhood a physical unitary character sufficient to differentiate it from surrounding localities. This, of course, will involve a systematic scheme of city planning. The following quotation indicates that this subject is already receiving consideration from experts on city planning:

There is then a need today, from the standpoint of city planning, for a standard political area corresponding to the city neighborhood—or if one answers that there are no such things as city neighborhoods, then for the city neighborhoods that ought to exist. A large city should be divided into local or neighborhood governments, presumably elective, which should, under the city government, have charge of certain physical interests of the district. The desirability of having real city neighborhoods matching certain city planning needs—and, though meeting these, realizing also certain spiritual ends—neighborhoods defined and vitalized by the possession accordingly of certain governing powers, is enforced in many ways.

It is emphasized by the monotonous lack of local structural design and thus of efficient organic character in our outspread cities, looked at as wholes. It is emphasized by the struggling efforts of groups of persons in various localities, through local improvement clubs, to affect their local physical conditions by their joint efforts, and by the fact that, as things are, a great part of the people feel helpless or indifferent concerning these matters. It is emphasized by projects which have been made by architects and sociologists to design fit groupings for local institutions, business, cultural and social, with a view for the better performance of their proper functions and a better symbolizing of the idea of neighborhood solidarity.

It is emphasized by the zealous and in many places locally rooted social center movement, which has spread so widely during the last few years. It is emphasized by the desire of finest elements of many isolated nationality groups for broad and inclusive co-operation in their districts toward social welfare, and by the spreading notion that common folk should be mustered into the life of the community as they have not been heretofore. It is emphasized by the recognized need for moderating the excessive and wasteful mobility of city populations, by giving more meaning to locality and making neighborhoods more worthy of permanent residence. It is emphasized by the fact that certain local interests, touching both the physical functions and social aims of modern government, can be better understood and administered locally than by the long range machinery of a city government centering at city hall and covering perhaps scores or hundreds of square miles. It is emphasized by the historical fact that the finest architectural embodiments of human institutions and ideals have for the most part been wrought out by communities of limited size, as ancient Athens and the cathedral cities of Europe amply testify.

As to precisely what functions would lend themselves to efficient local management—possibly the design, construction, maintenance and adornment of local streets, the removal of household waste, the provision of some recreation factors, especially for the smallest children, the receipt of taxes, the registration of vital statistics, the development of an architectural scheme for a real neighborhood center—whether these are some of the functions which might be considered as appropriate for local management, is a question upon which I do not wish now to enter. Nor need we now discuss whether this primary governing area should comprise one square mile or ten, 10,000 people or 100,000. Cases would be decided according to circumstances. Just as local intelligence, pride, and initiative, however, are invaluable in smaller cities for the purpose of government, just as the value of these forces is indicated by that fear of losing them which leads many outside communities to resist annexation to larger communities—so, I believe, these forces will, when given fair opportunity, demonstrate their value and efficiency toward limited city neighborhood government on a well-considered plan. I believe that the proper scope and objects of city planning will be neither adequately conceived nor adequately achieved except through the application to the large city of some federal scheme which will bring to bear the potentialities of neighborhood political areas as such for their own higher physical organization.[1]

However much we may idealize the values of the social solidarity of the traditional neighborhood and long for their return, the fact remains that our social order has changed profoundly from the organic life of the old hamlet or village societies. The seething movements of population show no signs of abating. Community life is ever growing more mobile and transitory. The demand for small homes or apartments, equipped with every possible built-in feature—if not completely furnished—is increasing. The modern family is loath to assume any responsibilities which may interfere with its freedom to move when opportunity or occasion arises. It is all a phase of the dynamic economic and social order in which we are now living. With the change undoubtedly we lose some of the values which went with solidarity, but, on the other hand, we gain much through the very looseness of the present social structure. Perhaps some of the neighborhood values may be restored by intelligent organization, but there seems to be little ground for belief that the dreams of the more extreme neighborhood promoters will ever be realized.

[1] George E. Hooker, "City Planning and Political Areas," *National Municipal Review*, VI (May, 1917), 341–42.